Dear Kathi,
  I really enjoyed
this book, it opened
my eyes to how
teen-agers & parents
feel. I hope that it
be of some use to you
          Love,
          Cathy

"LISTEN, MOM AND DAD ..."

Young adults look back on their upbringing

ORSON SCOTT CARD

BOOKCRAFT, INC.
Salt Lake City, Utah

Library of Congress Catalog Card Number: 77-79666
ISBN 0-88494-320-8

First Printing, 1977

Lithographed in the United States of America
PUBLISHERS PRESS
Salt Lake City, Utah

To Bil and Peggy Card
(alias Mom and Dad):
They told me that I was worth something
and then treated me
as if they believed it.

Contents

Preface

Parenthood is the world's most popular amateur sport. No matter how much you read, no matter how much you plan, your kids are going to have some surprises for you.

And you shouldn't be surprised at that! Listen, Mom and Dad: Your children come to you with a personality already. They are not a blank slate on which you can write what you want.

All you can do is teach us and guide us and limit us and love us and encourage us to grow emotionally, spiritually, socially, and mentally even while you feed our bodies so we'll grow physically.

Sometimes, even after the best treatment possible, some of us rebel. It will break your heart, for a while at least — but don't blame yourself for things that aren't your fault.

In fact, don't even blame yourself for things that *are* your fault. It's a lot better to spend your time figuring out how to solve the problems.

Many parents have a hard time communicating with their children. Not because they don't talk, and not because they

Acknowledgments

I owe a great debt to the many friends who have talked to me, formally and informally, providing the stories and the insights that appear in this book. For their sake I have disguised actual events enough that they probably won't recognize themselves. But the lessons they have learned and passed on to me they will surely recognize.

I also thank Jay M. Todd, who provided the initial push that got me into this project; Jay A. Parry, who read and criticized every page as soon as it came out of the typewriter, helping me to constantly improve; and my wife, Kristine, for not begrudging me the many hours I did not spend with her because I was working on this book.

And I also thank the mothers and fathers of the Church for having children. We never turn out quite the way you think we will, and sometimes we act as if we wished we didn't have parents to "interfere" in our lives. But take my word for it: we're glad you fathered and mothered us, and no matter how many complaints we may sometimes have, we love you, we're grateful to you, and we're glad that we'll belong to you forever.

aren't willing to listen, but because there are just some things kids don't often talk about to their parents. We children forget to tell Mom and Dad how much we appreciate the good things; or we don't want to hurt them (or ourselves) by telling them the things they do that we don't like.

This book is an attempt to tell parents — and grandparents, and young people who will be parents someday — some of the right things and some of the wrong things that parents do. The ideas presented here may be something you'll want to try — or something you'll want to avoid doing.

Don't misunderstand, though. This book isn't about communication.

It *is* communication.

So please, Mom and Dad — listen for a few pages.

Listen, Mom and Dad . . .

Introduction: I've got something to tell you

Parents — and future parents — your children have something to say to you. It's a message of love. It's a message of the great power you've had in our lives. We want to tell you how you did — how you're doing — at raising us.

Sorry. In preparing the book it was impossible to get together *all* the people in the world who have once been children and compare notes. But there are many similarities between the stories that young people tell of the way they've been raised. It is possible to generalize somewhat.

In the chapters of this book you will read the words of six characters: Todd, LaDell, Reuben, Arlene, Dave, and Cathy. You've never met them, for each of them is a composite of many people, with many experiences. But all the incidents they tell of really happened. As you read them, you may see yourself or your own children in the people told about and the people telling. If you see your own actions told about, weigh them carefully. If the results are good, then keep it up. If not, you may want to tone it down.

Each of the stories you will read has taken place many times to my knowledge, with only minor variations. Beyond my knowledge, I believe that each experience has happened to thousands.

Those thousands may include some young people living in *your* house. Their stories are taking place right now. Or tomorrow. Or last night.

Todd served a mission in South America and baptized almost a hundred people. He has been active in church all his life, earned his Eagle at the age of fourteen, was president of two quorums and an assistant in a third during his Aaronic Priesthood years. He was a good, though not exceptional, student. He now has his college degree, is married in the temple, has one child, plans on many more, and is serving as a second counselor in a bishopric. He is twenty-six.

LaDell is also married, with three children. She is a visiting teacher now, and also teaches Primary. In her spare time, which she rarely has, she still paints. She painted all through high school, to the exclusion of almost every other interest. She got into an art school, earned a bachelor of fine arts degree, and if she hadn't met and married her husband, she would probably have had a pretty good career as an illustrator or designer. She does not regret her choice. She is married in the temple, though she had never worried much about it when she was growing up. She is twenty-seven.

Reuben served a mission but didn't really enjoy it. It was hard work, he had little success, and he couldn't keep up much interest in it. Now he is back in college, where he is a senior for the third year because he has kept changing majors. Last month he changed his major again, but now he is sure that he has found his field. He keeps dating, and because he's a pretty good-looking guy girls get interested in him, but he hasn't found *the one*. Actually, he isn't really looking, doesn't even know what *the one* should be like. He goes to church most of the time. He does his home teaching regularly. But he doesn't really have a burning desire to get out and serve. At anything. He is twenty-five.

Arlene is not married. Arlene does not think she will ever get married. She is twenty-eight, a little overweight, but not worried about it much. What she worries about is the fact that in all her life, she really hasn't developed a close, binding relationship with anyone, male or female. She doesn't really know how to go about it. She has always been a loner, but she can't remember ever wanting to be. Her career is going well. She has no concern over her future security. But she is lonely, and resents the fact.

Dave also served a mission, and got to be a mission leader. When he sets his mind to something, he gets it done. He is vaguely aware of the fact that in tests back in school days his IQ was in the genius range. But he doesn't much care. He simply does whatever comes to mind and does it thoroughly. He has used drugs, and quit. He was once married, but it didn't work out and they divorced after a few months. He isn't bitter about it, really. It was just a mistake. He dropped out of college to take a good job and is now making more money than any of his friends who went to college. But he doesn't plan to stay in his job long. It's too boring. He believes in the gospel. He goes to church a lot. He usually dates LDS girls. He is twenty-seven.

Cathy is married to the man she had to marry at the age of nineteen. Now, three children and nine years later, they are almost ready to go through the temple. About four years ago, they almost had a divorce. But they returned to the Church instead, and began to value more what they had in their marriage. There are still problems, though. Cathy still feels trapped by responsibilities, and sometimes wishes she were free. She works as a secretary to help make ends meet. She is trying to be a good mother. Now the Church is a great support to her, but she remembers hating the Church for years. She hasn't had much contact with her parents since she got married. She wishes for more, but she is afraid to make the first move toward closeness; and so are they.

These are the characters who will speak the words and tell the stories of a generation of young people. These short biographies have said almost nothing about their childhoods. This is because they will tell their own stories, in bits and pieces, throughout the following chapters. Remember — the characters are fictional, but the stories are true.

Listen, Mom and Dad . . . these are your children speaking.

Listen, Mom and Dad . . .

1
what did you really want from me?

Children come as strangers into a strange land. They don't know the language. They have no control over the strange machine God has given them to live in. And they certainly don't know any of the local customs.

Parents are a child's first friends. They lead the way. They help the child learn to use his body. They teach him to talk, just by talking to him. And they teach him right and wrong, courteous and discourteous, kind and cruel — in short, what society and the family and the Lord want from him.

Sometimes parents teach these things deliberately. Sometimes parents don't plan carefully what they will teach — but the learning goes on anyway, sometimes in directions quite different from the parents' good intentions! And sometimes parents are so inconsistent themselves that their children don't know where to turn or what to do.

After all, the Lord said we must *teach* our children to walk uprightly before him. Children are born innocent, but unless they're taught they'll lose that innocence far too quickly.

Arlene

My parents expected us to do our part. That was really the most basic rule. It was even a family motto: "We all share the work and we all share the play." After dinner those who were assigned to do dishes did dishes. Those who had chores in the yard did chores in the yard. It was simply expected.

Even the two- and three-year-olds had to at least help whoever cleaned up their toys. Even if they could only pick up one toy at a time and had to be guided to the right place to put it, they did the picking up and putting.

I have very clear memories of drying dishes when I was so short I had to stand on a stool.

I also have very clear memories of not being able to play a game with the family because I had refused to help clear the table when I was asked to.

There was never any doubt of what was expected of us: participation. We were all part of making the home run smoothly. I guess that's why I'm such a compulsive worker now. I can't stand to be in the same room with an unmade bed. A dirty dish screams at me until I wash it. Dust on a table will keep me awake at night until I've dusted it. When there's work to do, I do it. It makes me a wonderful person to have on a committee.

Dave

Nothing was expected of us. It was that simple. Oh, the basics — toilet training, learning to feed ourselves. But my parents had the attitude that if you wait long enough, any kid is going to learn how to do what he needs to learn to do. They never rushed it. Some of us stayed in diapers a little longer than normal. Some of us couldn't dress ourselves until rather late. But they refused to push us.

They didn't really think of themselves, I guess, as shapers. They believed that each child would find his own shape, his own direction in life. Which is a fine theory, but let's face it — a kid is like any other animal, he's going to do things the easy way. The things we wanted to do, we did right away. The things we didn't want to do, we never did.

My parents thought of themselves as a resource. If we ever showed curiosity, they tried to have an answer. If we wanted to learn how to do something, they helped us learn.

The problem with this "letting kids grow up naturally" stuff is that the natural man is an enemy to God! Not really, not a little kid — but let's face it, little kids are completely selfish. They want what they want when they want it. I sure did. And because my parents never taught me patience, never taught me to wait for a while, or to not expect always to get what I wanted, I was absolutely impossible in kindergarten. I was a grabber. If I wanted a toy, I grabbed. If I wanted to be on the rung of the monkey bars where someone else was, I pushed him off. It took a very patient, kind kindergarten teacher to finally get it through my thick skull that the reason the other kids didn't like me was because I kept doing rotten things to them. Until kindergarten, I had always believed that the world revolved around me.

And that's a lousy thing to let a kid believe. Because it isn't true. And if he isn't taught to limit himself, the world will do the teaching the hard way. The hard way isn't any fun.

Cathy

There was only one expectation from my parents. Obey. Now and forever, obey. And do it fast.

Come meant *come now.*

And disobedience meant a swat or a lecture.

We never knew from one minute to the next what we were supposed to do. We didn't obey rules, we obeyed Mom and Dad. We just knew that if we didn't obey as soon as they let us know what was expected, we'd wish we had. It made us very attentive children.

The whole thing seemed very unfair. We never knew if what we were about to do would be punished or not, because we had no rules to go by. Very confusing for a child. I was very confused.

Reuben

When you're sixth out of seven, you don't worry about expectations. You learn really fast that if you're going to get any attention, you'd better make yourself heard.

I think child-rearing was almost an accidental by-product of everyday life in our family. All the older brothers and sisters knew the rules. I learned by osmosis. It was kind of like going to a strange country where you don't speak the language. You learn pretty fast just because if you make a mistake, nobody understands. In order to make a place for yourself, you have to learn the words. Maybe that's not a good analogy. But I pretty soon learned in my family that I had to get in line to use the bathroom, that if I didn't grab the food as it passed by I'd have an empty plate, and that if I did certain things either Mom or Dad or one of my older brothers and sisters would give me a swat. No one ever taught me the rules. I just learned them by living at home.

LaDell

The rules were always clear. The punishments always made sense. And we always knew why we were being punished. But as long as we stayed within the rules, we were given quite a bit of freedom of action.

One thing I really appreciated was that it was always assumed that I was a good person. No one ever called me a bad girl. My parents never treated me as if they assumed I'd disobey. I remember that even when they were toilet-training my little brother, they always acted surprised when he made a mistake. Yet they didn't get terribly upset. They reminded him what the toilet was for, and just assumed that he knew what he was supposed to do and that next time he would do it.

It was a good balance: surprised that we'd do anything bad, but not shocked. Disappointed when we disobeyed, but not furious. They always treated me like a person with a great potential. And when I didn't measure up, they expected me to go on and do better next time. And usually I did.

Todd

Mom and Dad expected us to be people. Of course they made allowances for the fact that we were just kids. But they always talked to us like adults. They expected us to carry on intelligent conversations. They insisted that we be rational and discuss things. If we argued with each other, they insisted that we sit down and discuss the disagreement without yelling or getting mad.

That was the way we lived. We talked about everything. We are a very verbal family. Corporal punishment was rare. We always talked things through. I was never in doubt as to what my parents expected, because if I had a question I could ask and I knew I'd get an answer. I knew that if I disagreed, they would listen to my disagreement. They took me seriously.

They expected me to be a person. Which is what I always felt like I was. I never felt like a child. Of course, there were firm rules and obedience was expected. But Mom and Dad always had a reason for the rules, you know. They made sense. The world was rational.

Listen, Mom and Dad:

1. We want to please you: just let us know what you expect.

2. If you give us no rules, we will be confused.

3. If we have no limits, we will have a hard time learning self-control.

4. If we are surrounded by arbitrary limits that we don't understand, we will have a hard time thinking of those limits as something other than just your whims.

5. We are capable of understanding and reasoning earlier than you might think. We understand language long before we can talk. We understand reasoning long before we act reasonably.

6. Your expectations can be self-fulfilling prophecies: if you expect us to be good, and let us know that, chances are we'll be good. If you expect us to be bad, and let us know that, chances are your expectations will be fulfilled.

Listen, Mom and Dad . . .

2
did you really
love me
as much as them?

We who had brothers and sisters have all felt sorry for those solitary children who have no siblings. But sometimes (when we couldn't get into the bathroom, when our possessions were used and damaged without permission, when we were pushed and pulled more than we thought right!) we wished *we* had been an only child.

If we were oldest, then anything that went wrong could be blamed on us (after all, you're older, you should know better!).

If we were youngest, then we got treated like children longer, and could never do anything the older ones did (just wait a few years!).

And those of us in the middle — we got it coming and going.

But then, thinking about what Christmas would have been like if ours had been the only stocking; about what it would have been like to have no other children at home to confide in; about what it would have been like not to have had a *family* around —

We wouldn't trade them in for anything else.

LaDell

Being the oldest in my family I really can't compare. I mean, I don't know what it's like to have an older brother or sister.

But it wasn't bad being oldest, really. In many ways it separates you from the younger kids — in other ways it draws you closer.

Because I was the oldest I was left in charge a lot. Responsibility came early — I was left in charge of the younger kids for hours at a time even when I was eight or nine. I was expected to keep them safe and keep them obedient to the rules.

Like once when my little brother climbed up on a rock and fell off and hurt himself. I hadn't even been left in charge — we were at a park and I was just playing near him. But my father — after he had patched up my brother's cut lip — asked me very seriously why I hadn't stopped my brother from climbing where it was dangerous.

"He wouldn't listen to me," I said.

"Then you should have called your mother and me."

This is one of the reasons why as the oldest there were barriers between me and my little brothers and sisters. When Mom and Dad were gone, I was the voice of authority. Sometimes they felt resentful. And I remember being really hurt sometimes because they played with each other but didn't always include me. This was because they felt like I was always "watching" them.

And I guess I was. I eventually had to learn the limits of my authority over them. It wasn't easy to learn it, either. Because we got in the habit of me telling them what to do and them having to do it. Even now I'll just decide something at a family gathering, and one of my younger brothers or sisters will have to say, "Whoa, wait a minute, we haven't all agreed on that." I get embarrassed, but they all laugh it off. An oldest child can just get in the habit of deciding and having the other kids go along.

Of course, that had some good effects, too. I've always been able to make decisions quickly, and they're usually pretty good decisions.

And in some ways being oldest does make you closer to the younger kids. Because they come to rely on you when they're in trouble. I remember when my little brother was thirteen he smoked a cigarette on a dare. He felt awful about it. And so he came to me and told me — not Mom and Dad, even though my parents are such reasonable people. He was ashamed to tell them. But me he could tell, knowing that I'd keep his confidence and have good advice. I advised him to tell Mom and Dad after he had prayed to the Lord and promised never to do it again.

In later years all the kids have come to me for help and advice. Sometimes the problems have been too big for me, or I just plain haven't had the answers — and I've told them so. But they still seem to have felt better for having told someone.

Kids can't always tell parents everything, because the parents' good opinion of them is so important. They don't dare risk it. But they can tell a brother and sister, and so find some kind of help.

And being the oldest, even my parents sometimes turn to me. I've been in on some private discussions and given advice on some things that the younger kids couldn't be included on.

I suppose that if I had been flighty and undependable I wouldn't have been relied on so much. But I also think that if I hadn't been relied on so much, I wouldn't be such a reliable person. I really gained a lot from being oldest.

Reuben

I wasn't youngest. I was next to youngest. But being the youngest kid is really a drag. Well, not always. But a lot of the time.

For example, when one of your older brothers is in a mood to fight with somebody, who's he going to fight with? Somebody older and bigger than him? Not a chance. It's good old punching bag Reuben who gets his daylights knocked out. I had one brother who always punched when he got mad. And there were times when I really feared for my life. I mean, those punches *hurt*.

Fortunately, my parents had a pretty low opinion of a kid who picks on somebody smaller than him, and so I could get help from them. But even that got me in trouble — the older kids would call me a tattle-tale when I ran to Mom and Dad for help. Sometimes I just didn't complain about getting picked on because I knew that if Mom and Dad did anything about it I'd just get it worse later on.

I wish my parents had been a little more aware of that, you know? When they walked in a room, and there I am in tears and there's my older brother looking mad, it's a pretty safe bet that something's going on. But my parents would ask, "Is anything wrong?"

Now what am I going to say, "Yeah, he's beating up on me"? Not a chance. Because I know that later on that day, if I tell on him, I'll get beaten up on even worse. Or else he'll refuse to play with me, which is the worst punishment of all.

Of course, it's just as bad when the parents walk into the room, see I'm crying, and automatically punish my older brother or sister. I mean, a younger kid's going to cry easier. Even if it's his fault. And so sometimes my older brothers and sisters got punished when it wasn't even their fault, just because I cried. And they didn't like me much when that happened.

And if I could get my parents to do anything differently, I would get them to never, never make an older kid play with a younger kid. When an older kid doesn't want to hang around with the squirt, and his parents make him, believe me the little one isn't going to enjoy the experience. The little kid's gonna pay for *every* bit of playing that gets done.

They always left me out, too. In family discussions, they'd say, "You're too small." They'd go horseback riding — I had to stay in the car. "You're too small."

The trouble is that the youngest kid is *always* going to be younger. I mean, if the parents just look around and see who's biggest, the little ones will always be left out. I think it would be a good idea for parents to keep a chart. On the chart they would have all the children's names along one side. Then along the top they should list all the things that kids do when they get to be a certain age. Like, "Ride a bicycle." And "Stay home without a babysitter." "Fix his own lunch." "Ride in an airplane." "Order his own meal in a restaurant." "Visit at friends' houses after school."

And then they should write down at what age every kid did those things. Now, I know that kids aren't always ready for things at the same ages. But sometimes the difference is ridiculous. Like one time I asked my oldest brother how old he was when he tended the rest of us, when he was left home alone sometimes. He was eight. Well, I was fourteen and my little sister was twelve when it finally dawned on Mom and Dad that they didn't really need to have someone stay home and tend us. Ridiculous, huh?

And Dad ordered my meals until I was twelve. An eight-year-old can't talk to a waitress? If you can pronounce the word *hamburger,* you can order a meal.

But it wasn't always a hassle, of course. It was nice that whenever somebody older than me and I did something wrong, he'd always get a bigger punishment than me "because he should know better." Whatever happened to him, I knew I'd have it easier. Ha! That's another thing that makes younger kids unpopular with the older ones!

Actually, my parents tried very hard to be fair. But it's absolutely impossible to treat kids alike. And really, we wouldn't have liked being treated the same. We're different people, you know? My brothers and sisters and I have all gone in different directions all our lives. It would have been horrible to have to do everything exactly the same. All in all, I'd say my parents did as fair a job of handling us kids as anyone could do. And being youngest wasn't all *that* bad.

Todd

My brothers have been really important in my life. Especially my next older brother Gary.

We had just about the normal amount of bickering and so on. We shared a room because our oldest brother got a small bedroom of his own and Gary and I got the big room in the basement, which was fun. We did a lot together, and we have a lot of our best memories in common.

But one thing that I really remember was how he learned to feel responsible for me.

The elementary school I went to when I was in first grade wasn't far away — easy walking distance. But to get there you had to go along this path through an orchard and then cross a bridge over a stream. The path had a fence on either side, and so did the bridge.

Well, while I was in first grade there was a bully there on the bridge. Now, I was small for my age anyway, and that kid figured I was great bullying material. He wouldn't let me cross the bridge. He grabbed me by my shirt and told me I had to go home. Finally he let me by, but I was absolutely petrified. The kid was a second grader, he was mean, and I didn't know what to do. He told me as I ran off toward the school that the next day he'd be waiting for me, and that tomorrow he'd really pound me.

Of course I told Mom and Dad. They decided that the best thing would be for Gary to walk me to school. Gary was in fourth grade then, and he went to school a half hour later than I did. He really thought it was stupid that a mere second grader would scare me (to him second graders weren't scary), and he really didn't like having to get up earlier in the morning to see me off and worst of all was having to be seen walking through the orchard with his dumb little brother (all little brothers are, by definition, dumb — when the older brother's friends are around).

So Gary grumbled all the way to the orchard. And then, when we got to the start of the path, there was one of Gary's friends. Gary was really embarrassed to be there with me. So he told me, "OK, you'll be all right from here on," and he walked away and left me there.

The trouble was, that he had only walked me through the safe part. It was the bridge where the bully was. But Gary told me not to be a crybaby and so there I was.

I went on through the orchard, and sure enough, there on the bridge was the bully. He remembered me. Of course. And he yelled at me about how he was going to pound me.

So I turned around and started to go back through the orchard. The bully left the bridge and chased me, and he caught me. When he caught me he punched me in the stomach. I cried. As soon as I cried he was satisfied and left me.

I walked home crying. Mother was really surprised to see me. She was really upset when she found out Gary had left me before we got past the bully. She left what she was doing and drove me to school.

That night Mom and Dad took Gary aside and gave him a long talking-to. Later on that night he came to me and told me he was sorry, but I could tell he was mad that he had gotten in trouble.

I really felt after that like Gary didn't really care about me. It was not a feeling that I could put into words. But I just figured that Gary didn't care what happened to me, so I'd better watch out for myself. And I didn't try to tag along with him anymore.

And Mom drove me to school for a few weeks, until the principal of the school installed a patrol guard on the bridge, besides the crossing guards who stopped traffic on some of the roads near the school.

But later on something happened that completely restored my confidence in Gary. It was during the summer, and Gary and I had gone to the store on our bikes to buy something for Mom. One of Gary's friends joined us on the way. Well, when we got outside afterward, Gary's friend started teasing me. He held onto the back of my bicycle so I couldn't go. I got really mad at him, and he just kept teasing me and calling me a crybaby (even though I wasn't crying). And when I got off my bike to try to make him go away, he pushed my bike over.

Just then Gary came out of the store after paying for the groceries and saw what was happening. He just walked up to his friend and grabbed him by the hair and said, really angrily, "If I ever catch you picking on my little brother again I'll pound you into the dirt." Then he shoved his friend away. The friend was really mad and yelled things, but he kept his distance from Gary and rode off pretty fast when Gary made like he was going to chase him.

Then Gary said to me, "Nobody picks on a brother of mine, the creep."

Somewhere along the line Gary had learned family loyalty. But after that, you can bet I would've died for him! I mean, Gary could say, walk across that wire twenty feet off the ground, and I would've done it just to have him think well of me.

Parents often don't realize how much that is really important to their kids happens when the parents aren't there. My brothers had a lot of influence on my life over the years. They taught me a lot of things. And even in a good, open family like ours, the most important things that went on between my brothers and me happened when my parents weren't there. Not that we were on our best behavior in front of our parents — that's a little much to expect. It's just that a lot of secrets get shared, a lot of games get played, where the parents can't see, not because we kids were ashamed, but because we thought our parents would think the games were silly, or because we just plain didn't want an audience. And that's what parents often are: an audience, not participants. They either applaud or boo the performance, and we kids cared very much which they did. But brothers — and I guess sisters, too, though I didn't have any — are really important to each other in ways that parents just can't be.

Listen, Mom and Dad:

1. No matter how hard you try to be fair, there's no way you can or should treat all of us kids the same.

2. However, *do* try to be fair.

3. Remember that the way you react to kids' relationships with each other may not have the effect you want — be careful you don't set one of your kids up to be punished later by his brothers and sisters.

4. And don't be jealous of our closeness with our brothers and sisters. They aren't as strong an influence on our lives as you are — but they're still strong, and that's the way it should be.

Listen, Mom and Dad . . .

3
I remember
every
spanking

Theories are as prevalent as green leaves in the jungle. Sometimes it seems like the great child-rearing question of the age is "To spank, or not to spank."

Well, that's not the question. Rather the question is the parents' general attitude. Dr. Diana Baumrind of the University of California at Berkeley divides parental attitudes toward discipline into three categories.

Authoritarian parents have the attitude that obedience is the first objective of child-rearing — as long as the kid does what he's told, he's a good kid. Such parents may spank, or they may not. Other techniques are to withhold their love and affection from misbehaving children, or to punish the children with verbal abuse. The manner isn't so important as that authoritarian parents are basically *punishers.*

Permissive parents have the attitude that children, left all alone, will turn into wonderful, creative human beings, and that parents are there only as a friend and resource for them. Such parents rarely punish. Instead they encourage their children, show them love and affection constantly, are careful always to be kind, whether the child is doing good things or not. Permissive parents are *rewarders*.

Authoritative parents occupy that vast middle ground. Sometimes they punish. Sometimes they reward. But most important, they tell the children which of those is happening and what the child did to deserve it. They listen to the children. Authoritative parents are *communicators*.

Cathy

I think my parents believed they were doing me this big favor by not spanking me. But there were times when I wished they'd just wallop me and *forget* it. Instead they yelled. And they never forgave, they never forgot.

You want me to be specific? I don't know, it was all the time, it's hard to think of an example — OK, I remember one, this was one of the worst. I think I was only five; I had to be five, I wasn't in school yet.

Mom took me shopping with her. I was too big for the cart and besides there were Teddy and Jimmy, and they were in the grocery cart, so I was walking. This was big time for me, five years old and walking along in the store like a person instead of riding in the cart like a kid. And I touched everything I passed. You know, the colored wrappers, the boxes, the cans, the price tags.

I really liked ravioli. We had ravioli sometimes, in cans, and I saw a can with a picture of ravioli on it and so, big grownup girl of five like I thought I was, I picked it up. Mom didn't notice, she was always looking at the list, and telling the two boys in the front of the cart to just be quiet for a minute so Mother can think, that kind of thing.

So we get to the checkstand, and I still have the can of ravioli. By then I had almost forgotten I had it. Mother had everything rung up by the lady, and Mom was writing the check, when the saleslady looks at me and says, really snide, "I wonder if you're planning on paying for your *child's* purchase, ma'am!"

I think back now, and I realize that Mother must have been really embarrassed by this, because the counter lady was really nasty about it, as if after spending twenty bucks on groceries Mom's going to conspire with her five-year-old to steal a twenty-cent can of ravioli! But Mom was really embarrassed, and she *jerked* the can out of my hands and said, really loud, "I'm sorry, ma'am, I had no idea my daughter had picked this up." And Mother paid the money to the lady and threw the can of ravioli in the sack and grabbed my hand and we took off.

As soon as we got to the car Mother started into a really long tirade. It's been so long, who can remember that long what somebody said? It was just over and over again, "your father and I didn't raise you to be a thief, don't you *ever* steal something like that again, don't you *ever* embarrass me in front of people again, from now on I'm going to leave you home when I go shopping or lock you in the car or tie your hands together with a strap" — I remember, that was the one that scared me. I had nightmares about being led through supermarkets with my hands tied together with a strap, being led by my mother. I could imagine people saying, "Why are your daughter's hands tied?" and my mother would answer, "Because she's a thief."

I cried all the way home, but Mother kept on talking to me like that, like she really hated me. I think back now, and I realize that she was probably just embarrassed and trying to teach me a lesson about it. I don't think she realized that I thought she hated me, but that's what I thought.

And then when Father got home she told *him,* and *he* came into my room and said, "Now Cathy, I'm not going to spank you, because I'm not a mean daddy." (He always told me how he wasn't a mean Daddy — what a joke!) "But when you take things that don't belong to you, that's stealing, and Heavenly Father gets angry at you." So now Heavenly Father was mad at me, too, and the truth of the matter was, I just thought I was being a big lady and taking things off the shelf like Mom did. I didn't know about *paying.* I didn't even know about stealing!

And then for weeks and weeks and weeks after that — it felt like forever — whenever Mother would go to the store she'd make a point of leaving me home, or leaving me in the car, saying, "I'd better not take you into the store, Cathy, and *you know why.*" And then, when she finally let me come in, she said, "Now Cathy, I'm letting you in this time, but you'd better remember about stealing. Do you promise not to steal anything?" I was so humiliated — every time, it was awful. And I promised not to steal.

You can believe that I didn't steal, either. I didn't even *touch* the stuff on the shelves. For a long time I didn't even *buy* things when I had *money.*

But here's the kick — when I turned thirteen and got into eighth grade I started hanging around with these kids who'd go shoplifting in teams. At first they had me spotting, you know, watching for the store cop. Later on I got to lift stuff. It was exciting, it was fun, and best of all, it was stealing.

I knew it was wrong, but it felt so — not good; but mean, like killing the mosquito that bit you, you know? — that's how it felt. Because all the time when I was a little kid my parents branded me as a thief.

And yet I think they were only trying to teach me a lesson. I don't really believe they knew how cruel they were being.

And it was the same thing, time after time. I came one time to the dinner table with dirty hands, for months afterward Mother herds me into the bathroom and washes my hands herself, calling me her "dirty little daughter." I get a C- in second grade reading, and suddenly after school every day I have to read and read and read, and all the time she's telling the neighbors how her daughter has a reading problem — she did this in front of me, too — and how she's helping me to stop goofing off and get down to the business of learning. You know something? I still can't read. I just can't ever get into anything. Oh, you know, I can *read.* I just can't read a whole book, or a whole article, I just start reading and I feel so antsy about it, I just put it down, switch on the TV, listen to the radio.

I just wish they would've spanked me. Anything. Beaten me. People feel so sorry for kids who get beaten by their parents. Boy, that's like a picnic compared to what I got. No, I know that isn't true, I'm really glad they didn't hit me. But if they had just *forgiven* me sometimes, given me a second chance, given me room to make mistakes.

Oh well. I've certainly made enough mistakes since then!

Todd

My parents weren't great spankers. I only remember one spanking in my whole life. I remember the whole thing, from beginning to end. It was during a time when my Mom worked, and so we were with this babysitter. She was German or Swiss or something and she didn't speak English very well and she just sat there in front of the TV. My little brother and I — after we got home from school, I was ten and he was seven, I think, something like that — she'd make us a snack: crackers, milk, juice, that kind of thing.

And then she'd go back to the TV and we'd just do whatever we wanted.

So one day we got into the drawer where the sharp knives are kept, and we got two of the neatest-looking ones and went out in the back yard. We tried throwing them at the wooden fence, but none of them would ever stick. And then my little brother threw too hard and his went over the fence into the neighbor's yard. So much for throwing knives at the fence.

So we went back into the house and got another knife for him, and then we decided to play knife fight. We decided we were gang leaders (this was right after *West Side Story* came out) and we were having a fight to the death.

It was fun. Having real knives made it exciting. And of course we both were only pretending — nobody was getting close to hurting anybody.

Until by accident my little brother moved his hand wrong and I laid his finger open. He just looked at it while the blood came pumping out, and I was scared to death, and he started screaming, and we ran into the house.

While the babysitter took care of my brother's finger — and it wasn't that bad, just bloody — I put the knives away. I made the babysitter promise not to tell how it happened. And then I got my little brother (bandaged finger and all) and told him to tell the folks that we were cutting things out and he cut his own finger on the scissors.

This was because I knew darn well that it was against the family rules for us kids to play with knives. And I knew that as the oldest of the two of us, I'd be held responsible.

So the folks came home, and the babysitter, who didn't speak English all that well, just said that my brother had cut his finger and that was that. I told the folks the story about the scissors and they believed me. Why should they think I was lying?

But all of a sudden, my little brother is the star. He has a hurt. Everybody pays attention. So he didn't stop talking about his cut. And as he talked, he just happened to slip and mention that it was a knife.

Then me, Todd the genius, I correct him and say, "No, stupid, it wasn't a knife, it was scissors."

"Oh yeah," he said. "Scissors. I forgot."

But my parents weren't stupid. They caught on. And they were very angry. But they just went into the bedroom and conferred about it for a while. Then they came back out. I almost remember this conversation by rote.

"Well, Todd, do you know what you did wrong?" my dad asked.

"Yes."

"What did you do wrong?"

"I played with knives when it was against the rules."

"That's right, son," Dad said. "And ordinarily, when I found out that you had played with knives when you knew it was against the rules, I would have been angry, and I probably would have put you on restrictions for a few days, so you'd remember." (Being on restrictions could mean anything from being confined to the house to being kept away from TV to being confined to my room to having to come straight home after school.)

I was feeling pretty good. Only restrictions. I could take that.

"But that wasn't the only thing you did wrong, was it?" Dad asked.

I really had to think about it.

"Todd," Dad said. "Todd, you lied to me. And not only did you lie to me, you told your little brother to lie to me, too."

"Yeah. I'm sorry."

"And you wouldn't have told me the truth if I hadn't caught you making a mistake. You would have gone on lying to me, wouldn't you?"

I nodded.

"Playing with knives is bad, because it's against the rules. But lying to your mom and dad and getting your little brother to lie, too — that's much, much worse. That's breaking a commandment, did you know that?"

I knew that. I wasn't dumb. I knew the Ten Commandments from Primary or Sunday School.

"So your mother and I have decided that I'm going to have to do something to help you remember never to lie to us again. Will you come with me to the garage?"

I was so scared. Not that I thought I'd get terribly beaten. But because I felt like the world was ending. My parents were disappointed in me. Maybe that doesn't seem like such a big thing, but to me it was. It still is, if you want to know the truth. I really hate it when they're disappointed in me.

But I was scared. Dad took me out into the garage, and he took a flat, flexible metal ruler from its hook on the wall, and he explained to me again why he was going to have to hit me, and made me say back to him why I was being punished. I was crying by then, and I said, "Daddy, please don't spank me."

I'm not a coward. But it just felt like if Daddy spanked me it would be the end of the world.

But Dad just said, "Son, I can see that you really feel sorry. But if I didn't spank you now, you'd just figure that whenever you did something wrong, all you'd have to do is say you're sorry and then everything would be all right. I'm glad that you feel sorry about lying. I hope you feel so sorry that you'll never do it again. But you still have to be spanked."

And so he had me kneel down over a box, and he gave me maybe three swats. They were sharp, and they stung, but really they didn't hurt that bad. And yet they hurt worse than anything had ever hurt me before in my life.

When he was through I was crying really hard, and Dad put his arm around me and he said, "I really love you, son, and I believe you're a good boy and you're going to grow up to be a good man. Will you remember from now on to tell your mother and father the truth?"

I nodded.

Then he gave me a big hug and asked me if I wanted to go back in the house. I said no because I was still crying or almost crying and my eyes were red and I just didn't want to be around my brothers right then, because even though they wouldn't have said anything, I would have been embarrassed. So I said, "Please no."

So Dad stayed with me out in the garage for a while. We didn't play together and have a fun time — the mood stayed serious — but he showed me some things and we talked about some things until he saw that I was calmed down and he said, "Are you ready to go in now?"

"Don't let anybody tease me," I said.

"I won't let anybody tease you," he said.

And he didn't. And that's the only spanking I ever got. Except maybe when I was two and I don't remember that.

But that's something, you know. Mom and Dad never punished me without explaining to me what it was they were punishing me for.

Right now I suppose you're thinking that I never told another lie. That isn't true. I lied other times, to try to get out of trouble at school, things like that. But to Mom and Dad — well, when I lied to them it really stung, it made me feel bad. And so I almost always told them the truth.

Dave

My parents figured I was a smart kid. They didn't try to push me around. What I did was OK with them. They usually tried to give me advice. You know, "Dave, don't you think it would be better if you helped your father mow the lawn?" I said, "Sure." But then I didn't help him mow the lawn, and they didn't say much.

"Don't you think it would be a good idea if you told us where you were going after school, Dave?"

"I just mess around."

"We'd really like to know what you're doing."

"I'm doing *nothing*," I'd say, getting irritated. "I'm all right."

And they never really pushed anything.

One thing they always said: "Son, if you ever want to talk to us about anything, if you ever have a question, you can ask us, you know that, don't you?"

"Sure," I always said.

I think they were trying to communicate with me, or something.

But the funny thing is, I really hated it. I really could do anything I wanted. I could stay after school and mess around. I remember one guy, he always had to call home. His mom always gave him permission to goof off with us, and still he always called. I one time said, "How come you always call home when you know she's just going to say yes?"

He just shrugged. "She just wants to know. She worries."

That's what got me. I didn't think my folks worried.

Since then I've found out that they worried all right. They stayed up late talking about me, worrying about me, wondering what I was doing. But they didn't want to repress me. I'm a genius, you know. The IQ tests and all that. Don't look at my grades, my grades keep my IQ a secret. But see, they figured they had this genius son, and they had to be careful not to interfere with my creativity. My Mom told me only a little while ago, she said, "We always thought of you as a special gift from God, as someone precious. We were always a little scared of you."

Well, to tell the truth, I was always a little scared, too. I used to think when I was a kid, if I dropped dead right here, nobody would notice for a week until the school called my parents and reported that I had been absent and was I sick. I used to go to a big creekbed that was usually dry and play around in the culverts that went under roads; it was kind of scary and dangerous. And I'd think, what if there was a flash flood right now? I'd be swept away, and no one would even care. "Is this Dave's mother?" they'd ask on the telephone. "Well, we just found your son's body in the San Francisco Bay." And I imagined my mother saying, "Oh, so that's why he wasn't home for dinner. Well, box him up and send him home, I guess we'll have to have a funeral."

I know, that sounds funny now, and I even laughed then, but I really felt bitter about it. I won a debate meet in high school, the state debate meet, me and my partner took first. We got together at the debate coach's house for refreshments afterward and everybody else was calling their parents and telling them, and somebody noticed that I wasn't calling *my* parents, and here I had the biggest win of the meet. I tried to shrug it off, but they kept asking, "Why don't you call your folks?"

So I said, "Nobody's there who'd give a damn."

That shut them up. But I believed it. Since then I've had experiences that told me they *did* care. But all my growing up years I felt lost. Lonely. Even though I had lots of friends and went everywhere with them in grade school, I still felt like I just didn't belong anywhere.

I'll tell you a secret. I still don't feel like I belong. Really, I don't feel like I belong much of anywhere. I'm just kind of drifting. Really kind of too bad, huh? What a waste of an IQ. God should've given it to somebody who'd do something with it. Here I am feeling sorry for myself. What a joker I am.

Arlene

I always obeyed my parents. They never had to punish me. I would always think before I did anything, would Mother like me if she saw me doing this? And if the answer was no, I didn't do it.

And I always helped out at home. I'm the oldest girl, and my mother had this idea that women should do the work in the house, and men should do the work outside the house. So I helped. I came home after school and helped make dinner, or tend the kids. I'm a great little homemaker. My Dad used to say, "Someday you'll make somebody a wonderful wife." So, when is someday? Ha ha. That was meant to be a joke.

I always knew when my mother was upset at me because she'd just get cold and silent. It was little things — short answers when I talked to her, maybe closing drawers in the kitchen a little louder than usual, refusing when I offered to help. Then I'd sit there and wonder what did I do to make her mad. I really got worried. And it could go on for hours, just her being cold to me. Not the silent treatment, she'd speak to me, things like, "Would you be willing to pass me the butter, Arlene?" things like that.

That was it. She'd get polite. And then, sometime in the next few hours or the next few days, I'd find a note on my dresser. It would be really cryptic. Something like, "In the future, please don't bring home friends without giving me enough advance warning that I won't be humiliated by the condition of the house." Then I'd think back and remember that I had brought a friend home and there was some stuff stacked in the living room.

One of the notes — it was really almost funny, thinking back on it — it said, "When we are so rich that we can afford to have cookies made out of ingredients that need to be used for sustenance, I'll start giving you ten-dollar bills for lunch money." See, I had made some cookies as a surprise for the family.

But from then on, I always asked. I practically asked permission to *breathe* — no, I'm getting sarcastic, I'm sorry. It's just that it was so impossible to *talk* to mother. I just walked on eggshells for fear I'd hurt her feelings.

My father never criticized me. And my mother never praised me. Sometimes I was scared to come home. And yet when I finally moved away from home it was the hardest thing I had ever done. I didn't know *how* to make decisions. Mom had always made them for me.

Reuben

I remember that Dad used to give spankings that made the rafters ring. I'm the sixth of seven, and I remember when Dad got mad at the older boys, they got hit from heck to breakfast.

But when I was seven, I remember that my brother Jay, he was sixteen, he just decided he wasn't going to stand still for it anymore. It's kind of a family joke, now, among us kids, but we don't talk about it in front of Dad or Jay.

Anyway, I don't know what Jay had done, but he had a flip lip, and Dad got mad, and all of us were kind of getting out of the way so we wouldn't have to watch the spanking — but when Dad reached out for Jay, Jay just took off. *Nobody* ever took off. We learned really young that the spanking was always easier if you just stood there and took it like a man and then walked bowlegged the rest of the night. But Jay took off.

Now our kitchen and our living room and our dining room and our family room were kind of like a circle, with the hall going off one end toward the bedroom and the bathrooms. But Dad chased Jay around and around from the kitchen to the dining room to the living room to the family room to the kitchen. It was almost funny there, for a while, and Dad and Jay even laughed, but finally Dad started getting tired and he yelled and told Jay to stop, he was tired of playing games, and Jay just said, "You can lick me if you can catch me, old man."

And then it wasn't funny anymore. Mother kept saying, "Please, stop this, please Jay, please Daddy, just stop this." But Dad ignored her.

Finally Jay took off down the hall and locked himself in the bathroom. Dad stood there against the door, panting, and said, "Open the door, Jay."

Jay didn't open the door.

"If you don't open the door, and I have to break it down, you'll wish you'd never been born."

And Jay yelled back, "I wish I'd never been born to a Dad like you!"

So Dad kicked in the door. It splintered the doorjamb and cracked the door from top to bottom and ripped the handle out. It wasn't a very strong door.

And then Dad went into the bathroom. He looked so mad. Mother was still saying, "Please stop," and one of my older sisters was crying, and Jay looked scared to death, and then Dad started hitting him, not with the flat of his hand on his backside or anything, I mean really punching him out. Dad had gotten in some fights in the army in World War II, but this one — Jay didn't even have a chance, though he tried to defend himself. Dad just kept punching and punching until Jay was lying down in the bathtub screaming with his nose broken and his lip split and a black eye and Dad suddenly stopped. Mother just looked at him for a minute and then said, "You animal!" and she gathered up all us kids and took us out of the house and drove us around and around and took us to the park. When we got back the doctor was just leaving and Jay's nose was bandaged and Dad was in his and Mom's bedroom.

Now we laugh about it, because it was so funny there for a while, Dad chasing Jay around and around. But it wasn't really funny at the time. Anyway, something happened to Dad when he saw what he did to Jay when he really got mad, and from then on he never laid a hand on one of us again. When Dad repents about something, he doesn't kid around. From then on it was getting grounded, stuff like that. So since I was seven, I've never been spanked.

LaDell

It was simple enough in our family. We had rules, and every few weeks in family council we'd go over the major ones, like never calling brothers and sisters names, and always doing what Mother and Father asked unless we had a real reason, and then explain the reason, and things like that. Whenever there was a new rule, or one of us thought a rule wasn't fair, we'd talk it over in family council, and change it or not change it. We never voted. But when Mom and Dad made a decision, we knew why it had been made.

And punishments were always pretty sensible. I mean, if you stayed out too late on a date, you had a curfew the next night of an hour earlier than before. Or when we were little, if we took a toy away from one of our brothers and sisters when we knew it was their toy, why, we had a few toys taken away from us for a while. And I can remember Mother even talking to one of the younger kids when he couldn't even talk much yet, and explaining, "Now Ryan, you don't pull the books out of the bookshelves. That's because you might hurt the books, and because the shelf might fall on you. Here's where there's some paper you can play with. Whenever you want to rip things up, you can play with this paper. But when you take books off the shelves, I have to spank you."

Can a kid that age really understand? I don't know. I just know that I always grew up talking to my parents and having them talk to me, and I never felt that they were being arbitrary. They always were trying to be fair. Sometimes we thought they weren't fair and they went ahead with the discipline anyway. And we'd pout and think what rotten parents we had. But we knew where we stood. And as long as we weren't breaking a rule, they let us make our own decisions. I really like the way my parents handled discipline. That's how I do it with my kids. It takes the patience of Job, believe me. But I think it's worth it. I want my children to feel about me the way I feel about my parents.

And you know? Whenever we really obeyed all the rules, they'd change the rules to make them more lenient, because — and they told us this all the time — "When we know you are trying to do the right thing, we'll let you make your own choices. But when you keep trying to do wrong things, then we can't let you make choices." Once we had lost a privilege because of breaking rules or doing something really dumb that we knew better than to do, after a little while they gave us another chance.

Like I said — they always seemed fair.

Listen, Mom and Dad:

1. When you've got to punish us, explain why.

2. Let us know the rules in advance. Don't make us guess whether what we're doing is right or wrong.

3. Don't, please don't, ever let us think you hate us or think we're rotten people because we've done something wrong. Punish us, but let us rise afterward.

4. If you can't control your temper, don't punish or reprimand your children until you aren't angry anymore. We can only interpret your anger as hatred.

5. Let the punishment fit the offense.

6. Don't make us bleed. Nothing is worth inflicting real pain on your children.

7. Let us repent. Forgive us when we have repented. Trust us again.

8. Let us appeal. If we don't think you're being fair, at least listen to us.

9. But do make rules. Don't leave us loose without a rudder. It's too scary to be totally free.

Listen, Mom and Dad . . .

4
I had
opinions,
too

So much of a child's life is determined by things completely out of his control: the neighborhood he lives in, the school he attends, the church he learns to go to, even what he's going to have for dinner. When the child is young he has virtually no control at all. But later . . .

It's a dilemma for parents. How much voice should the children have in the family decisions? How much freedom should they be allowed in their own decisions? What do children have to do to earn their parents' trust or distrust?

One important thing to remember is that children do not think of themselves as young. They only think of themselves as small. Their desires and thoughts and opinions are *every* bit as real to them as yours are to you. That doesn't mean that they are equally right: the child with the opinion that it doesn't matter whether he runs out into the street without looking or not is definitely incorrect. Nevertheless, *he* won't automatically see that. And when a child believes that his parents don't care what *he* thinks when they make decisions that affect him —

Well, he might just come to believe that his opinions are worthless. And if his opinions are worthless, then maybe . . .

Arlene

The first time in my life that I ever really had to make decisions on my own was when I went to college. I was totally unprepared.

My mother was so careful of me (there are *men* in the world who are just waiting for young girls to be alone) that I really have no memories of solitude outside my home until I went to college. I was simply not allowed to go anywhere alone. And almost always — I believe always, but I have to hedge, you know, to avoid being unfair — *almost* always the person who was with me was either Mother or Father. I never went anywhere with just my friends, because in grade school, when I had friends, we always had an adult along, and in high school I had no friends. The farthest I ever walked alone was to and from school — as long as we lived where there were no large streets between home and the school. Even then, if I wasn't home by *exactly* ten minutes after school was out, Mother would panic and start calling everybody. It only took two times of the principal coming into a school class where I was staying after to talk to the teacher or some other students, announcing that my mother was wondering why I wasn't home; I never lingered after school again.

I didn't buy my own clothing without my mother there to veto anything she found unsuitable until I got to college. Even then, I agonized over every clothing purchase, wondering what my mother would think.

In restaurants, even when I was in high school, Mom and Dad felt free to contradict my choice in front of the waitress. My father didn't like eggs unless the yolk was hard. Therefore I didn't taste a fried egg with a soft yolk until my first meal at a restaurant after I got to college. It was like a holiday. I ordered a milkshake, fried eggs sunny side up, and a hot dog. It was probably the strangest meal I ever ate — but it felt so good to be eating things that I had *never* been allowed to order (at your weight, milkshakes will do you no good, dear; and hot dogs — you never know what's in a hot dog in a restaurant).

When I got to college I was really quite pathetic. Fortunately, I had a very understanding roommate who gradually helped me learn some basics: like decent taste in clothes and how to fix my hair so it looked reasonably up-to-date in the late sixties. She even introduced me to historical romances, not exactly high class, but still — Mother had refused to let me read trash like that. Imagine my disappointment when I found out how really drab those exciting forbidden novels were!

That same roommate, bless her soul, refused to make any decisions for me. I remember asking her, time and again, "Well, what'll I do now?" At first she'd make suggestions — but pretty soon she caught on to the idea that I was automatically doing what she suggested, just as if she were my mother. So then when I asked what I should do, she'd say, "I don't know. What are the options?" She made me list what choices I had. I had never learned to choose alternatives.

Now, maybe I've given you the impression I was completely stupid. I did make some normal choices, like what order to do my homework in, things like that. But I was, compared to other children, tied down and staked out.

I remember in second grade, when I really realized for the first time that other children actually went and visited each other at each other's *home.* I went home and asked Mom if I could go over to somebody's house and play.

"Who?" she asked. Well, I didn't have anybody in mind — I was just asking about it in general. But I picked a name, a girl in my class.

"Where does she live?"

I didn't know.

"Out of the question."

But she seemed so agitated by the very request that it was a long time before I asked that again.

I guess I'm running this into the ground. Let me just say that I realize my parents were prompted entirely by a concern for my safety. Well, perhaps they also wanted to avoid the inconvenience of having to live with any mistakes I might make. Anyway, I know they loved me and thought they were doing the best thing.

But the growing-up years are supposed to allow a child to mature, to become capable of getting along as an adult in the world. When I first plunged out into the world — if you can call BYU the world — I was as helpless as a preschooler. If there's a decision-making muscle, mine had atrophied from utter non-use.

Todd

My parents had pretty strict rules. Not all that many of them, I guess. But the rules they had, they *meant.* When they said, don't hit your brother, that meant don't hit your brother! I found that out the hard way. I didn't even hurt him — I mean, it was my *older* brother. But Dad saw me, and I was confined to my room for the rest of the evening.

And yet — my parents knew when to let infractions slide. I know, that's against all the theories. But what policeman would arrest you for speeding when he found out you were rushing somebody to the hospital? I mean, there are exceptions, mitigating circumstances to almost any rule. Even ''Thou shalt not kill'' isn't held against you in wartime.

A lot of parents don't know when to look the other way, though. I've seen some of my friends' parents take it personally if the kids broke a rule. I'm glad my parents were mature enough to realize that breaking the rules did not mean that I didn't love my parents.

I didn't break many rules. But there was one rule —

When I was nine we moved to a house that backed right onto a creek. Normally the creek was dry, at least in the summer. But whenever it rained the creek quickly became a torrent. If it rained heavily, the creek flowed right up near the top of the banks — at least twenty feet deep, with murky brown waves tumbling violently along. And sometimes there could even be flash floods, when it stormed in the mountains.

So we had a strict rule: we kids were absolutely forbidden to climb the back fence and go into the area of the creek.

Now, my older brothers were all caught up in school activities, and my little brother was only six. At the age of nine, I really felt pretty alone.

But that didn't bother me. I know this might sound funny, because I guess that I seem like a pretty gregarious guy. But there are still times when I get this kind of melancholy mood going and I want to be alone, to daydream, to think. Well, I spent a lot of time when I was nine doing just that.

And in my search for solitude, it wasn't enough just to be alone. I had to be alone and *secret,* alone where no one would know where I was. Don't ask me why, because I really don't have that need now. My wife would get pretty upset if I did!

But I took to climbing that back fence. And I went down to the creek. And I built a fort.

Before I left the yard, I'd check to make sure Mom was busy and my brothers weren't likely to notice. Then I'd clamber up the fence, hop over, and go down to the creek. When I came back, I'd peek through the knots in the fence to make sure the back yard was empty, and climb back over when the coast was clear.

I built my fort by putting old boards between the trunks of two trees growing out of the side of the creek. They wobbled, but once I was on them, they were sturdy enough to support my nine-year-old body.

I've also got to admit that part of the attraction of that place *was* the danger. Several times I went to my fort only a little while after a storm, when the creek was still running about three feet deep. Then my fort hung out over the water. I would lie there and look down at the roiling water. It was stirring, that's all I can think of to call that feeling. I felt stirred.

In that fort I fancied myself invisible — and I really did a pretty good job of camouflaging it with branches and stuff. I mean, it was pretty obvious that there was a fort there — but it wasn't easy to tell that someone was in it.

It was in that fort that I first read Tarzan and a series of civil war and revolutionary war novels for children. The librarian probably would have had a fit if she could have seen the books dangling over the creekbed as I read. But I never dropped a book, and what she didn't know didn't hurt her.

And I dreamed. Lay on my back looking up at the leaves. Watching the wind. Thinking.

It was a good time.

And then fall came and I went back to school and only got to the fort every now and then. That winter an especially bad storm sent a current through the creek that ripped out one of the two trees, and the fort was gone.

During that storm, Dad went over the back fence to check on the water level — we were worried that the house might be flooded. I begged and begged to be allowed to go with him. Finally he said yes, if I promised not to let go of his hand under any circumstances. I promised.

So we stood together about five feet back from the bank as the tree swayed in the current, tore away from the bank, and sailed majestically down the creek.

"Too bad, son," Dad said, squeezing my hand.

It wasn't until a long time later that I realized that his sympathy then meant that he knew perfectly well about my fort. Then I thought back to that summer. How my parents made it a point to tell me, every now and then, "Hey, Todd, look at the sky. That's probably a storm up in the mountains. Might mean a flood."

I never took it personally until later. And then I realized that they were aware that I was breaking that ironclad rule about the creek and the back fence — but they recognized my need for solitude, and didn't want to interfere. They even had the sensitivity to realize that I didn't want to know — at least at the time — that I *had* their permission. So they didn't weigh me down by granting it. And so they gave me the happiest summer of my life.

I probably worried them to death! I have to admire their self-control in *not* stopping me.

Dave

My parents were real child psychologists. Many times during my childhood I heard my parents agree to the most outlandish requests from their children with the words, "All right, dear, we don't want to stifle you." Apparently they viewed us all as fragile, delicate butterflies who would be stifled by rules and limitations. They would warn us, "Careful of that busy street," and grab a little kid who might be running right toward the road — but they'd never make a *rule* like, Don't go in the road.

But along with their grant of freedom to us kids there was another grant of equal freedom to them. Of course it was never defined that way. But it was just taken for granted that we kids couldn't possibly have any objection to a decision *they* made about *their* lives — after all, they didn't stifle *us* did they?

It boiled down to live and let live. We kids pretty well did what we wanted, though the communication level stayed high in the sense that they knew in general what we were doing. And they did what they wanted, too.

Until the day that Dad came home and announced that he was quitting his job and accepting an offer in another state. It meant more money and infinitely more prestige, and he and Mom immediately began planning the move.

Trouble was, I was in junior high and Val and Annie were in high school. The little kids were excited about the move — but for us it was the end of the world, especially for Val, who was just heading into his senior year.

I don't think my parents really thought they were doing anything thoughtless or cruel. It was just so obvious that this move was the best possible thing.

Well, we kids talked about it and Val and Annie and I decided that moving this year was entirely out of the question. That's a pretty heady thing for three kids to decide, but you've got to remember that we were used to making our own decisions and doing what we wanted, and — I admit it — we were pretty darn selfish.

But at dinner one day, as Dad talked on about the houses he had looked at in the new area the weekend before — he had flown down — Val piped up and said, "You won't need six bedrooms."

"Why not?" the folks asked.

"Because Dave and Annie and me aren't going."

Wow, what a bombshell. I really think it was the first real confrontation in our family. Maybe not. But Dad and Mom listened — incredulously, believe me — as Val explained that since he was going to be captain of the debate team and the only possible leading man for the school's production of *Oklahoma!* it was completely unfair to make him leave for a high school where he'd be a total stranger. It would hurt his chances for a scholarship, too.

Then Annie put in her two-bits' worth. She was just the right age to start dating, she knew a whole bunch of boys in our ward and stake, and if she went to the new town she'd be a wallflower and an old maid right when she was reaching her prime.

My reasons were that I didn't want to go because I was going to get Miss Shipley's class the next year and she was a good teacher and I had too many friends to want to leave.

Mom and Dad were flabbergasted. If it had just been me or Annie, they would have laughed it off. But they couldn't just

laugh off Val's objections to the move — they really did make
sense.

Besides, they weren't in the habit of saying no to any of
their kids. And here we were, fully half of us, saying no to them.

We didn't discuss it any further at dinner. But the parents
were obviously upset — and hurt, too, I think. All their en-
thusiasm for the move just vanished. And yet it really was the
best possible thing for Dad's career; it would have been stupid
to pass it up.

And so we finally did something that had never really
happened in our family before: we got together and worked out
a compromise that everybody was happy with. We made a
decision together! It wasn't the start of a trend, though. Just a
one-shot deal.

What we did was, we made a list of the pros and cons of
going. There were some pros in the favor of us kids that we
hadn't thought of — like, it was a warmer climate and we could
swim year-round, there were more Mormons and so we'd be a
lot closer to the Church, the schools were better, things like
that. The swimming pools made irrevocable allies out of the
little kids, and pretty well won over Annie and me, too. Besides,
let's face it. When my reasons for wanting to stay were written
down, they looked pretty stupid even to me. And Annie knew
perfectly well that she was a knockout and guys would fall all
over themselves to date her no matter where she was.

(By the way, that's an interesting sidelight: why Annie
waited until she was sixteen to date. I'm pretty sure my parents
wouldn't have stopped her if she had wanted to date before
sixteen — my parents weren't much at drawing the line. But
Annie heard it in church so much that she decided on her own
that she would follow the prophet. That's maturity if you ask
me!)

But no matter how you put it, Val really would be ruined by
moving. And Dad would be set back if we didn't move.

Both Val and Dad were getting mad. And so finally I said the obvious thing that had been ruled out right from the start (Dad had begun the discussion by saying, "Whatever we do, we have to do it together"): I said, "Look, why don't we just find a place for Val to live here in town for his senior year and then the rest of us can move."

Out of the question. Nonsense. Said Mom and Dad.

Sounds all right to me. Said Val.

And Val put it on the line. "You never say no to me anyway. So I already do whatever I want. The only difference is that you won't be around here to watch me do it. So what?"

That really hurt my parents' feelings. But it was true. And then Dad and Mom agreed that it seemed like the only possible solution. We had a family prayer over it, and everybody went to bed.

And so Val stayed there and the rest of us moved and nothing bad happened and we promptly forgot that we had discovered it was possible to make decisions as a family. Too bad.

Cathy

I'm a pretty strong-willed person. In my family you had to be to survive.

A few weeks ago I was walking through a store with a friend, and we happened to see a lady walking along dragging a kid. The kid passed a toy department and tried to stop. The mother ignored the attempt and dragged the kid farther on.

Then a few minutes later we saw the same lady at a jewelry counter. The little kid kept trying to pull away from the mother — obviously because he was bored stiff. But the mother pulled him back really violently — the kid couldn't even sit down or anything, just had to stand there *facing* the counter, which was just bare wood, I mean, there was nothing to look at.

Finally the mother jerked the boy back so violently that he smashed his nose into the counter and started to wail. The second he started to cry she shook his arm and said, "Be quiet," in this hideously angry voice that sounded like she hated him. But he just kept crying. She spanked his bottom and told him to shut up. He just cried harder — not illogically, I don't think. Finally she turned to the saleslady and said something about how sorry she was that her child just didn't know how to behave. Then she picked the kid up roughly and walked out of the store in a huff. We could clearly hear her telling the boy, "Just you wait until I get you home."

My friend turned to me and said, "Can you believe that?"

I looked at her really blankly and said, "Can I believe what?"

You see, to me there wasn't anything unusual about that little scene. That could have been my mother. That could have been me getting carried out of the store — just twenty years ago.

That's the way it was, growing up with my parents. It wasn't so much that we kids had to obey rules. It was that we had to obey my parents. And that's a whole different thing. I mean, when there are rules, you know what to expect, right? And if you haven't broken a rule, you can't be punished, you know? But when all you have to obey are your parents, then you never know what's going to bother them. Anytime they get irritated, you get punished. Whatever they wanted to do, if you resisted, you'd really catch it.

When Mom said we were through playing in the park, we were through. I mean, right that minute we had to drop what we were doing and head for the car to come home. If we asked Dad for permission to do something, if he was in a bad mood the answer was no. Period. It didn't matter that you had done exactly the same thing the week before and nothing had gone wrong. If Dad was in the mood to say no, the answer was no.

We kids got to be experts at gauging our parents' moods. If Dad was quiet, *stay away*. If Mom was acting busy, *pretend you don't exist*. But if Dad was talkative, then maybe he was safe to ask for favors. If Dad was singing, then he'd say yes to anything. If Mom was sitting down or lying down, she'd probably say yes just to get rid of you. And if Mom was working — but calm, moving slowly, not acting busy — then she'd at least listen to what you had to say.

Welcome to the wonderful world of insecurity.

That's one of the reasons it was so hard for me to take them seriously when I was a teenager. They'd say, "It's not good for you to wear your skirts so short." And I'd say to myself, "That just means *you* don't like short skirts." They'd say, "It's against Church principles for you to date before you're sixteen," and I'd answer, "Sure, blame it on the Church."

I wasn't used to right and wrong entering into a discussion. I mean, my parents always used right and wrong when they told us no — but we kids knew perfectly well that what was "wrong" or "dangerous" or "foolish" or "bad" today might be perfectly acceptable tomorrow — and vice versa.

It wasn't until I learned the hard way that right and wrong are absolutes and not just whims that Mom and Dad thought of that I started being able to make wise decisions. Until I really got smashed up, until Larry and I were looking at the possibility of divorce, I really hadn't put one and one together and realized that some things I was doing were actually *wrong*.

That's why I'm so careful to explain things to my kids. I know that sometimes I'm arbitrary, I have bad moods like anybody else. But when my kids say, "But Mom, that isn't fair," then I listen. I really listen, and I decide sometimes, yeah, Cathy, that isn't fair. And so then I apologize and stick to the rules — not my whims. It isn't easy — but it isn't that hard, either.

LaDell

I remember family councils. My parents had family councils even when I was only three and not really aware of what was going on. But we'd sit down and Dad would say — half jokingly — "All right, the family council is now in session. The chair recognizes Mommy."

"I move we have dinner at Hungry Joe's."

"Do I hear a second?" Dad asked.

And then I'd bellow at the top of my three-year-old voice, "I second it!"

And so we'd go to Hungry Joe's.

Of course, in really important things, or things that involved money, Mom and Dad made the decision alone — when we were little. But I remember that when I turned eight, Dad made a big thing out of it. Not only was I being baptized and confirmed a member of the Church — I was also being made a full-fledged voting member of the family council.

I didn't understand that at the time, but as the years went on it became clear. When we bought new drapes for the living room, Mom and Dad would look at the fabric swatches in family council. I was perfectly free to say, "Yucko, I hate that one," to any of the fabrics. And that fabric was immediately put out of consideration. Unless, of course, I was saying that to *all* the fabrics, in which case Dad would say, "You're just being contrary" — and then they'd stop paying any attention to my statements at all, until I proved that I could be rational again.

And when the decision affected me particularly, I really got a hearing. Like the time when I wanted to repaint my bedroom. I wanted to do it in purple. Mom and Dad said, "All right, bring it up in family council."

So at the age of about eleven I explained to my brothers and sisters — and to Mom and Dad — that purple was my favorite color and I wanted a purple bedroom.

Then Dad and Mom patiently explained that the curtains in my room were green, as were my bedspread and my chair. It would be very costly to replace them, and they would look hideous in a purple bedroom.

I disagreed, saying that I wanted a purple bedroom and I thought green and purple looked good together.

So Dad and Mom voted that we should postpone the decision for a week.

A week later I still wanted a purple bedroom.

And so Dad and Mom put it to a vote. They voted no, and so did my brothers and sisters. I voted yes. I was really disappointed — I started to cry. But Dad said, "Wait a minute. There's something else to consider. The bedroom is LaDell's. None of us has to sleep in it — she does. So I move that even though we all disapprove of LaDell's choice, she be allowed to paint the bedroom purple on Daddy's next payday."

It went to a vote, and I won that time — over Mother's advice. She kept hinting that she hoped I'd change my mind and do something reasonable.

But I painted the room purple. Daddy helped me by doing the masking and reaching the high places. And they were absolutely right — it looked hideous. But Dad and Mom had stipulated that since paint was expensive, and we could only afford to repaint one room every six months, it would be almost four years before I could repaint. They warned me in advance that if I didn't like purple, that would be just too bad — for four years.

So for four years I had the most hideous bedroom you can imagine. It was dark, it was gloomy, everything clashed with the walls, I hated it. I wouldn't invite my friends into the room because they always laughed at my purple walls.

Mom and Dad never said, "I told you so." They had left the choice up to me. But after that, I listened a lot more carefully to my parents' advice.

Most of the time, anyway.

Of course, there were still some things that the majority didn't decide. Family rules for example. But even then, we could appeal them in family council. For example, once Mom and Dad had a rule that no one could turn on the television on Saturday morning until all the chores were done. Well, I always got up early on Saturdays and did my chores. And so I was ready at nine o'clock to watch Rocky and His Friends. But my little brother always slept late and dawdled around. I just didn't think it was fair that I had to sit there on Saturday morning and miss my TV show just because he wouldn't do his work. When I complained, Mom said, "Well, then, maybe you should help him." I tried that — but it just meant I ended up doing all my work and all of his, too.

So finally I brought it up in family council. I got really emotional about it, too. And when I was through with my impassioned declaration of why I thought the rule wasn't fair, Dad looked at Mom and Mom looked at Dad and then Dad said, "You're absolutely right. If Mommy agrees, then I say we'll change the rule so that whoever finishes their chores can watch TV right then in Mommy's and Daddy's room. Whoever hasn't finished their chores is not allowed in the room, period. And the first person through with her chores (he said *her* because I was always the first person through) gets to choose all the programs until eleven o'clock."

Mommy agreed.

And my little brother started doing his own chores. Fast.

But sometimes my parents simply vetoed. Like when I tried to get the family council to approve my going on a trip with some friends to Yosemite. True, there would be adult supervision. But Mom and Dad didn't know them, and the truth was I didn't know even the girl my age all that well. I just wanted to go to Yosemite. Dad and Mom refused even to let the family council vote on it. They just said, "That is the kind of thing that I'm surprised at you for even suggesting. You know the rules, and there's no reason for this to be an exception."

But they didn't say that until they had heard me out.

We kids kind of joke about it now that we're all pretty much grown up — whenever we arrive at a decision of any kind, we always say, "The Family Council is adjourned!" just like Dad always does. Like at a picnic, when somebody says, "Let's eat," somebody else always says, "The Family Council is adjourned!"

But we really do still hold family councils. Even though some of us are grown up and married, we're considered members of the council, and when we're home we sit in and help decide. And Jay and I are already holding family councils with our little ones.

It was in family council that I learned how to make decisions. Since I had to plead my case, sort of, it helped me learn to think clearly.

Listen, Mom and Dad:

1. We only learn to make wise decisions by making them. If we are never allowed to make decisions, we'll never learn how.

2. However, we should only be allowed to make the decisions that are within our reach. Without rules and boundaries, we can feel pretty lost.

3. Even if we are dead wrong, hear us out. If you've listened before you say no, the negative answer is easier to take.

4. If you are occasionally willing to change your mind, be a little flexible, it will help us to learn the same kind of wisdom.

5. Make rules and stick to them — except when prudence suggests that the rule should either be tightened or loosened in a particular case. If we have nothing regular to depend on, we lose our concept of right and wrong. Even the Lord doesn't rule by whim, though he does allow high considerations to make rare exceptions to lower laws.

6. Whether you use a regular family council or more informal procedures, the door should always be open for our opinions to be expressed.

7. And if you tell us we have a choice, don't renege when we
   choose unwisely. If you aren't willing to abide by the conse-
   quences of our choice, don't offer the possibility!

5
I needed
you
to care

The kids may *act* like they don't care what you think. The little ones may continue drawing on the walls even after you've asked them a dozen times not to. The middle ones may constantly forget to do their chores, no matter how often they're reminded. The teenagers may flout your standards and break your hearts until you're sure they feel nothing toward you.

But it's all a lie. When we did those things, when children do them now, we aren't saying "I hate you," even though there may be terrible moments when our lips actually say the words. What we're saying, deep down inside, is:

"What are you going to do about it, huh?"

And even deeper inside us than that, we're saying, "Don't you care about me? Show me that you care about me."

Reuben

Let's face it, when you're number six out of seven kids, you've got to work pretty hard to have anybody notice that you're there! When I was five or six, my older brothers and sisters were in junior high and high school and one was even in college. I mean, there were important things going on: graduations, dances, engagements (two of my sisters were married before I got into junior high), dating, scholarships, football and basketball and all that stuff. And what was I doing? See Dick Run. Run, Dick, Run. No wonder nobody noticed me!

But to *me* it was the dating and the football and all that stuff that was trivial. I mean, what's the big deal if Deanna is going out with some idiot guy tonight? I *still* want to tell somebody about my turtle. You know?

So I found these ways of getting noticed. I still have to laugh to think about it — but it worked.

Like the time I got under the dining room table and used up a whole roll of masking tape, taping shut the place where you pull it apart to put in the leaves. Then I forgot it — and about two weeks later my Dad and one of my brothers spent four or five minutes struggling with the thing until somebody got under the table and found the tape. They were absolutely sure that the catch was stuck, and my Dad made some nasty comments about the furniture company. After he found out, he made some nasty comments about *me*. But for a minute there, I was the star of the show.

Or the Christmas when I wrote "hi" on a whole bunch of pieces of tape and stuck them on *every* present in the house. It wasn't until half the presents were opened that somebody noticed the little message. Then *everybody* noticed them and some of them got so irritated that I had "ruined" their beautiful wrapping jobs. I just said, "I decided to spread some good cheer." And again I had everyone's undivided attention for a few minutes.

I would have hung by my feet from the ceiling if I thought I stood an even chance of having somebody come up and say, "Hey, Reuben, I notice you're hanging from the ceiling. How come?"

But sometimes I did the most bizarre things and no one even noticed. I once wrote "Boo!" on a piece of paper and stuck it in my parents' bed. Not a word about it afterward. Or the time my oldest brother was giving a sacrament meeting talk and I got into his carefully prepared notes and inserted a sentence saying, "And, brothers and sisters, I am a full-fledged idiot, and so are all of you." I sat there all through his talk, waiting for the moment when he'd see that sentence and at least *pause*. He went on without a pause and never mentioned my insertion afterward.

But after enough of them graduated and went on missions and got married, people started to notice. Mostly because I was almost the only one left. Then I cut out the clowning.

Dave

My parents really *tried* to act interested in me. But that's just it: I always knew they were acting. There's one phrase that I sometimes wanted to rip out of my parents' mouths the minute they started to say it: "How nice, dear." I have been how-nice-deared about three billion times in my life, and *every single time*, without any exceptions whatsoever, "how nice, dear," could have been replaced by the phrase, "Go away, I'm busy," without any change of meaning.

OK, so maybe what I was doing wasn't as important as what Mom and Dad were doing. But they could have looked up and for fifteen seconds actually noticed what I had done.

How many times did I hold something up for Mom or Dad to see it and have them say, "How nice, dear," without even glancing at it. I'd even *say*, "But you didn't *look*." They'd just answer, "Yes I did, dear, and it's very nice. Thank you for showing me."

Somewhere they had read that parents are supposed to give favorable responses to all their children's accomplishments or enthusiasms. What nobody told them — or at least it didn't sink in — was that the favorable responses needed to be *responses*. They had to be *sincere*. They really had to look at what I showed them, listen to what I told them.

After a while I gave up. I just got used to the fact that my parents really couldn't care less what I did. In more recent years, of course, I've learned that they cared very much. They were just being thoughtless. They just didn't realize that I wasn't stupid enough to be fooled by their repetition of that meaningless phrase.

I turned the tables on them, though. When I was about eighteen I remember Dad coming home from work announcing that he had just been made chief cook and bottlewasher of some big division of his company or something. Mother was just jumping out of her skin, she was so excited. I walked in and asked what was going on. Dad told me, and the truth is, I really was excited. But my nasty streak took over and I just kept on walking through the room and said, exactly the way they had always said it to me, "That's nice, Dad." And then I left.

Man, did that make me feel good. It was all I could do to keep from laughing out loud when Mom came in and talked to me privately in my room later that night and said, "Now, Dave, you really hurt your father's feelings. This promotion is very important to him, and you acted just as if you didn't even care." And after she left I did laugh. At least I think I was laughing.

Arlene

Right after I got my Ph.D. I came home for a few weeks. During that time I caught the flu and stayed in bed a lot. After being sick for four days or so I kind of felt better one night about eleven, and I got up and fixed myself a sandwich. I fixed it in the kitchen and didn't bother turning on a light because the moon was shining in the window and, I don't know, I kind of like sitting in the dark sometimes.

So I was sitting there eating the sandwich when my parents came home from wherever they had been. They must have figured I was in bed asleep — a good guess, since there weren't any lights on in the house. So they sat down in the living room to talk.

I should have coughed or something to let them know I was there. But by the time I realized I shouldn't overhear the conversation, I knew I could never let them know I had overheard it. More or less they were talking about how I was going to be an old maid.

Dad was saying things like, "She's got such a cold personality, no wonder guys don't ask her out. She acts like they were animals that she should wash her hands after touching. I mean, there are some decent guys in the world. And now she's *Dr.* Hansen. What guy in his right mind is going to go out with somebody named *Dr.* Hansen?"

Mom agreed with him completely and talked about how if I'd just control my eating habits and exercise and use some sense about the clothes I bought, I wouldn't be half bad-looking. And there I sat with a sandwich in my mouth.

"Well, let's face it," Dad said. "Right now she's downright ugly. And a girl's got a responsibility to look beautiful. I mean, how can you sell the merchandise if you wrap it in wilted lettuce? Sure, she's got a great mind, but who wants to take a mind to a movie?"

It went on after that, but I got up really quietly and dropped my sandwich in the garbage and then walked softly back to my bedroom and went to bed and cried.

I shouldn't have felt so bad about it. I mean, it meant that they really cared about me, they were concerned about my happiness and all that. I'm *glad* they're concerned about me. I just wish they liked me, too.

LaDell

One of the nicest things about my parents is that they always let me know that I was important in the family. For instance, when something really good happened to me at school, I never had to brag on myself to my younger brothers and sisters. All I had to do was tell Mom or Dad, and then at dinner they'd be so excited and *they'd* tell the other kids. It was so much more fun to have them tell it. Then I could just sit there and look modest. I know, I'm making it sound like a joke, but it wasn't, it was so *fun.* They made such a big thing out of all the good things that happened to me.

I knew they loved me because of little things like — well, like the time I took a little clay sculpture that I had done about a month before and used it as a basic model for a larger bronze work I was doing. It hadn't been out of the living room for more than a half hour before Mother came downstairs to ask me if I knew what had happened to it.

I showed her what I was doing, and she looked so relieved. "Your father walked into the living room and noticed right away that it was missing. We were so afraid that one of the little kids had broken it and then hidden the pieces so we wouldn't know, they know we'd be so upset." And as she left, she said, "Now you make sure you return that to us, that belongs to us, you know."

Can't help but make you feel good.

But when something important happened that *wasn't* good they were exactly the opposite. Not that they didn't pay attention — I mean they just didn't make a big thing about it. I once heard a visiting teacher tell my mother all about her own daughter's illegitimate pregnancy. I was absolutely appalled. If that woman's daughter had had any idea that her mother was talking about her like that — well, I would have just died.

But my parents never, to my knowledge, said anything critical about me to anybody who didn't have a right to know. And sometimes not even then!

Let me tell you one time. It was one of the most terrible experiences of my life. I was in a department store — I guess I was fifteen — and my parents were somewhere else in the store and I was looking around in the perfume department and found something I liked, but then I opened my purse and counted my money and realized I didn't have enough, so I put the perfume back and closed my purse and went to find Mom and Dad. They were already coming to find me, and we were all set to go home, and then just outside the store a man came and took me by the arm and said, "I beg your pardon, young lady, I'm a store detective and I need to have a word with you."

It took me a minute to catch on that the man thought I had been shoplifting. I looked at my parents and they looked so *shocked,* just incredulous. But the man insisted that I should follow him into the store. On the way to the office he asked me my name, and asked my parents their names, and at that time my Dad was bishop and the store detective said, "You're the Mormon bishop, aren't you," and of course Dad said yes, and by then I was just so embarrassed because — well, you know how it is, it's like when a policeman pulls you over to tell you that your back door is partly open. Even though you *know* you didn't do anything wrong, you get this sick feeling that somehow you did something and you're going to get in trouble for it.

Anyway, we finally got to the office and the man said, "Please open your purse." So I opened my purse and there were all my things. And nothing but my things. I spread everything out over the table and let's face it, sometimes you can be embarrassed by the kind of thing that ends up in your purse. But when the man saw what was there, he looked really confused. He looked at what I was wearing and realized there was no way I could hide anything in my clothes. He asked if he could look at my jacket pockets. Empty. And then he said, "I thought I saw your daughter pick up some perfume and drop it in her purse. I must have been mistaken." I told him he definitely was, but he looked so embarrassed that suddenly I felt sorry for *him* and I said that it certainly could look like that, that anybody could have made that mistake, I guess I babbled on like an idiot.

The man seemed really afraid, too. But Dad just patted the man's shoulder and said, "That's all right, we're glad to have the chance to remove any kind of suspicion on our daughter, you were just doing your job." And then we left.

Out in the car I just started to cry. Mom and Dad understood, of course, because it had been so terrifying for me. I asked them please not to tell anybody what had happened and they promised they wouldn't, even though they told me that since I hadn't done anything to be ashamed of, it wouldn't hurt for people to know. I was just so embarrassed and it had been so awful that I insisted that nobody know it.

And they never told anybody. But all that night, in little ways, they would just give me a pat or a squeeze or a smile or a kind look, just little things that helped me eventually calm down. And that night they came into my room and asked if they could have a special prayer with me. Mom said the prayer, and in it she thanked Heavenly Father that their daughter LaDell was the kind of person who they could be sure would never do anything wrong on purpose, and how grateful they were that never for a moment had either of them thought that I had actually taken anything. I was grateful for that, too. And then they prayed for the Lord to help me be calm and not feel bad about the experience.

They always let me know that what happened to me was at least as important to them as it was to me, whether it was good or bad. It's a wonderful thing to know your parents feel that way.

Listen, Mom and Dad:

1. To let us know you care, all you have to do is really pay attention.

2. It's even better when you care *and* we feel like you're on our side!

3. And when we misbehave, especially if we make no effort to conceal it, you might check back to see if you've been ignoring us lately!

Listen, Mom and Dad...

6
about you
and me
and school...

Some kids loved school. But to others it felt like slavery. There was nothing we could do about it. Carted off in the morning by our parents and *left* there. Abandoned. Without hope, without friends, in the power of strangers who forced us, all day, to perform ridiculous tasks and be quiet while doing it.

At night they let us go home. But the next day —

And it went on for years and years and years.

Off and on through all the grades of school, many children have a fleeting desire to grab their parents, shake them hard, and yell, "How could you do this to me!"

Dave

In about fourth grade they gave me what I now realize was an IQ test, and after that I started being given special projects. Advanced work. When I got to college I checked and found out that my IQ was pretty high. And it was always easy to get A's.

So officially school shouldn't have been any problem. The teachers and I got along pretty well — good students, let's face it, are rare, and even though a few teachers felt threatened by me, most of them went out of their way to help me.

I got along OK with the other kids, too.

So officially, like I said, school was no problem for me.

Actually, though, I was scared of it.

Most of the time it was routine — get up in the morning, eat breakfast, go to school. You never question it, you just do it.

But during first and second grades I had a terrible time with tardiness. I was always late. I'd leave fifteen minutes early from home, and it would take me thirty minutes to make the ten-minute walk. The teacher would comment on it, and finally made me take notes home to my parents. I took them home, and my parents, good old easy-going Mom and Dad, said, "By the way, Davey, your teachers have mentioned that you haven't been getting to school on time." That was it.

Finally it got so bad that the teacher sent me to the principal. That was terrifying. But all he did was talk to me and ask me why I didn't like to come to school on time.

He was a very nice man. I told him that I didn't know, but that I just didn't like to come.

And then he explained to me that even though I didn't like to come, I still *had* to come, and there was nothing that he or I or anyone could do about it, that was the law. So as long as I had to come anyway, I might as well come on time, thereby avoiding extra problems.

He made sense to me. From then on I was only late about once a week.

But several times during my school years my family moved. And then my fear of school would really get awful. My parents always moved at the end of summer, because we kids would always plead, "Oh, please let us have one last summer with our friends." Actually, it might have been better to move at the beginning of the summer so we wouldn't feel like such absolute strangers in the new place.

Anyway, every time we moved I went crazy on the first few days of school. I'd wake up in the morning feeling absolutely petrified. Not sick at all, just scared. So I'd lie to my parents and say I was sick.

Mom did the whole temperature bit, but even though the thermometer invariably read normal, I did such a good act of being ill that they'd let me stay home.

The second day I'd still be sick. And both those days I'd lie in bed all day so filled with anxiety that I couldn't sleep, couldn't concentrate on reading, couldn't do anything except just be anxious.

Finally, on the third day I'd decide not to be sick, because let's face it — I knew I couldn't keep up the pretense forever or my parents would start taking me to hospitals to have me checked and somewhere along the line a doctor would tell my parents that I was just shamming.

So I'd go to school. And just like it was when I was late all the time in the first few grades, it was much, much worse being a new boy in school on the *third* day than it would have been to be new on the first day. Everybody stared. All the desks were taken. All the early friendships had been started and I was out of it.

It would be every bit as bad as I had been afraid it would be.

Why was I afraid of school? I don't know. I think I was born with an instinctive desire not to be controlled by an institution. Or maybe because my parents were so easy-going, the rigid rules of school life scared me. Or maybe I'm just basically shy, I don't know. I just know that going to school was bad news, and nobody but that principal in my first-grade days ever seemed to understand that.

LaDell

I always loved school. I've never understood how anybody could hate it. That was where I made all my friends, except for my Sunday friends, who I met in church. School was where all the exciting, important things of my life were happening. You know — adults have all kinds of plans, all kinds of things to accomplish, deadlines, projects. The house, the yard, things like that. What does a kid have to give her a sense of accomplishment, to give a purpose to her life? School.

So I looked forward to the next day, I did my homework on time, I did extra credit things — I guess partly because I'm a born "accomplisher." I have to always be accomplishing something. And school provided the opportunity.

But that doesn't mean I'm not *normal*. Just like an adult sometimes wakes up in the morning and thinks, "If I have to go to work one more day I'll go absolutely crazy," even when they have a good job that they like, sometimes even a kid who's happy in school wakes up in the morning and says, "I think I'd rather die than go to school." You just get the mungies.

Well, my Mom and Dad understood that. And so we had a kind of standing agreement at home that every once in a while, when we just couldn't face a day of school, we could say so and Mom and Dad would let us stay home. Now, the rules on this were strict: we could never miss a test, and we could never stay home to have an excuse for turning in an assignment late. They always insisted that we fulfil our responsibilities. But if there wasn't anything vital going on in school that day, at least that we knew about (and our relationship with the folks was always pretty open — I can't remember lying to them very often; now and then, but not often), then we could stay home.

And there were other stipulations, too. Like, if we said we were sick and we really weren't, then we were bundled off to school anyway and punished for lying. And we couldn't do it very often, either, because Mom and Dad felt that education was absolutely vital. But within the limits they had set, we could occasionally have a day off.

Those days were always so good. Thinking back, I realized that they were anything but a vacation for poor Mom, having a wide-awake, active kid at home on her hands, but she always used the time so well.

We didn't get to play all day, because Mom made it clear that she had work to do, and if we played, we played alone. That was exactly what I wanted to do sometimes, of course, and I remember a few of those days just spent lying around reading or building with blocks or plastic bricks or drawing — especially drawing.

Television was limited to one hour, period. So that we never spent the whole day watching TV.

And if we were going to be with Mother, we had to help. For instance, once when I stayed home Mother had to bake cookies for the Relief Society for something-or-other. And so when I wanted to be with Mother, my time was spent rolling out the dough, cutting the cookies, watching through the glass door of the oven to be sure they didn't burn, and so on.

The best thing about helping Mom was that she didn't just give you the boring jobs. Even though she cared very much that the cookies look right, she didn't insist on cutting them out herself. Instead, when I cut a cooky out wrong, she'd point out the flaw, have me reroll the dough, and let me do it again. The first time it meant that it took longer to bake them. But later on, it meant that by the time I was nine I could start from scratch and follow a recipe from beginning to end and turn out reasonably good cookies.

Another time I stayed home from school, Dad had the day off, too, and I helped him wash the car. And I really *worked,* too.

Other times I worked alone. Once when I was in my early teens, I spent a whole spring day, when all my friends were in school, just weeding and fixing up the yard. I picked up garbage from all over, dug up every dandelion in the lawn, edged, trimmed, pruned — it was great. The next day I went to school with aching muscles and a vivid sunburn. Everybody wanted to know if I had been out boating or something. Nobody could believe that I had stayed home from school just to work in the yard.

I guess my parents were great believers in the work ethic, or something. But then, so am I. And because of them, I never felt like I was *forced* to go to school; and yet, on the days I stayed home I never wasted my time. I learned even more on the days I missed school than I did on the days I went.

Reuben

Not everybody is going to get *A*'s. I mean, *A* means superior, right? So for somebody to be graded superior, he's got to be superior *to* somebody.

I'm the guy they're superior to.

I'm not stupid. I never flunked out, I got only a few *D*s, I got more *B*s than *C*s. I even got an *A* now and then.

But my report cards were nothing to brag about.

But so what? You know? Is the world going to end just because my parents happened to have a kid who's average? Is there anything wrong with doing "satisfactory" work? — that's what *C* is supposed to mean, anyway.

It's one thing that I thought was really unfair about my parents when I was a little kid. Because all through grade school, I'd get punished for my grades. No, they never beat me over it or anything. But they'd make a real fuss over my brothers and sisters who got good grades, and I'd just get ignored. Or after report card time Dad would make this big deal about how he couldn't go here or go there at night "because I've got to help Reuben with his homework, he's having problems with his grades." I wasn't having problems with my grades. I was doing all right. I'm just not a genius.

And when I had to go without my bicycle for a whole quarter because I got a *D* in mathematics — I thought that was really rotten. Because I was only nine years old and dividing with fractions was *hard*, and taking away my bicycle didn't make dividing with fractions any easier.

My folks probably thought that by grounding me they'd make me study more. It didn't work. It just made me hate studying and hate math even more, because math had made me lose my bike. And I don't believe a person can do well in a subject he hates. That's what I think.

Arlene

I had no friends in high school. I never dated in high school. No one said *hi* to me in the halls, none of the other kids ate lunch with me, I was completely and totally alone.

But my parents always thought school was so great for me because I got such great grades. Of course I got great grades. I had nothing to do at school but study. Straight A's. What an accomplishment. I would have traded them all in just to have had somebody to eat lunch with.

My parents never realized that there was something wrong when their daughter always came straight home after school. They just thought I was well-behaved.

And I did get a college scholarship. The day I got it I cried myself to sleep. Because everybody in the family was so proud of me, and all I could think of was that I'd go to college and it would be four more years just as bad as high school.

I hated high school because I hated myself in high school.

Todd

I remember Mr. Emerson, my science teacher in eighth grade. He was acutely aware of the fact that I'm Mormon, and he liked to make little comments. They were always friendly comments, or at least wry humor. And he showed me by many things he did and said that he really liked me and respected me. He just thought that the fact that I was Mormon was cute.

But the thing I remember best about my year in Mr. Emerson's class was that that was the year we studied evolution. I remember being really disturbed by it, because I was sharp enough to make the connection between the idea of cavemen and the idea of Adam not being exactly compatible. At least, one story or the other had to give at *some* point to make them fit.

And Mr. Emerson, when he was teaching the lesson, made one of his little jokes. He said, "So that means that everybody here is descended from — not apes, remember — but from an early primate that resembled apes more closely than we do. That is, everybody except Todd, and he's descended from Brigham Young." Everybody laughed, including me, because it was funny.

But I was worried about evolution. And I remember asking Dad about it. He gave me a great explanation. I remember it especially, even though it wasn't the only time he talked to me about the things I learned in school, because it epitomized his whole approach to thinking. He didn't just say, "Evolution is wrong, the Bible is right," and so on and so on. Which was a good thing because, let's face it, I'm pragmatic enough that I just can't ignore the geological evidence — it isn't going to go away. So this is what he told me:

"The theory of evolution is basically that living things change over the years because things around them change — for instance, if there's a general drying out of the climate, then the flowers that can grow with less water will survive, while flowers of the same species that tend to need more water will disappear, and pretty soon all the flowers that are left will be the kind that don't need as much water. They'll be different from the way the species used to be. That's evolution.

"But most scientists assume that this is the *only* way that changes occur in species, and I don't think they have enough evidence to assume that. Now, a lot of Mormons accept different amounts of the theory of evolution. Some Mormons believe that evolution is just an out-and-out lie, that there's another explanation. But frankly, Todd, I don't think that any of their explanations really answer all the evidence.

"Some Mormons go to the other extreme and say that God must have used evolution to create everything, including man, and that somewhere along the line God picked out an animal that was almost like man and said, 'This one is Adam,' and gave him a human spirit. That's what some Mormons believe, but I really don't think that squares with the scriptures, because I think they're pretty clear about saying that the Lord created something special with Adam and Eve. Besides, the changes in each stage of evolution are so gradual that when one creature was exactly right to be called Adam, and made a man, that man's father would have been only so slightly different that the difference would have been unimportant. That would mean that there would be animals that wouldn't be men — but that you couldn't tell from men. I don't think the Lord works that way."

So then I asked Dad — and of course, you realize I've probably added to his words over the years, but that is pretty much what he said — I asked Dad what *he* believed. And he wouldn't tell me. He just said, "What I believe right now is my own opinion. But if I told you what I believe about it, you'd tend to accept it just because I say so, and I want you to think for yourself. So study both the scriptures and the schoolbooks, and you come to me and tell me what you think."

So I did that, and came up with some ideas of my own, and came to him and told him what I thought. He discussed it really seriously with me, raised some questions I hadn't thought of before, and sent me back to study even more.

Now I realize that what Dad was doing was teaching me how to think. He was teaching me to make sure I had reasons for what I believed, in those areas where the answers aren't absolutely crystal clear from scripture or from other revelations given to the Church. I mean, about faith and repentance and the divinity of Christ and things like that, Dad left no room for doubt, and he would bear testimony to us about it, and we knew exactly where he stood. But on things like evolution and politics and economics and areas where it wasn't a matter of testimony but rather a matter of opinion, Dad made sure that we kids had a doggone good reason before we made up our minds.

I remember he always told us, "You don't have a right to have an opinion until you've asked yourself all the questions."

It turned out that I ended up with a different idea about evolution from the one Dad had. We talked about it, and it turned out that I was more "orthodox" — I stuck closer to the literal scripture account. And over the years, Dad eventually changed his opinion until it was closer to mine.

When my kids have questions about what they're learning in school, that's the way I intend to handle it.

By the way, when Mr. Emerson gave us the test on that unit in science class, he had an essay question about evolution, and as he passed out the test he made it a point to say, "Now Todd, all I want you to write about is what we studied. Don't give me any extra opinions because I don't want to have a lawsuit over freedom of religion." He said it with a wink and everybody laughed.

But when I was through writing the answer he wanted, I spent three more paragraphs telling him what *I* believed. And when I got the test back, he had written along the bottom, "Todd — almost thou persuadest me to be a Mormon."

Good teachers, you know — both Dad and Mr. Emerson.

Listen, Mom and Dad:

1. If we're afraid of school, our fears aren't just something childish, to be dismissed by saying, "He'll outgrow it." School can be terrifying.

2. Even if we like school, sometimes it can be a drag.

3. Don't make us feel ashamed if we're doing our best and our best is only average. Even average people, if they're right-eous, can enter the celestial kingdom. Can't we?

4. Don't panic when the gospel and our schoolteachers teach different things. If you handle it right, the experience can really help us grow.

Listen, Mom and Dad . . .

7

about
the
Church . . .

Children of Latter-day Saint parents learn about the Church very young. Church is where Mom and Dad always are. Church is where they have to sit still for years and years until sacrament meeting is over. Church is where they learn about Jesus and Jonah and Moses and Joseph Smith.

Church is where they throw spitwads and play basketball and gossip on the back row.

Church is where they learn to want to go on missions, to get married in the temple, to pray, to serve.

But sometimes church is just the place where Mom and Dad make them go every Sunday.

Dave

Maybe if my parents had insisted that I attend every meeting I might not have drifted away from the Church the way I did. But, to tell the truth, I don't think it would have mattered whether I was taken to every meeting on Sunday or not. Because church bored me silly, and I just plain hated to go.

I admit, I'm not the usual case. Usually kids are bored with church because they don't understand or because they don't care. Now, when I was a kid I really did care about the Church. I cared so much that when I was ten I was the only person I knew who had read all four standard works. I had read them carefully, too — at least, I could answer all the questions in the game "Seek" without referring to the answer sheet!

The trouble was, I kept having Sunday School and priesthood meeting teachers who just plain didn't know as much as me. There's nothing more irritating in the world than spending a whole class period watching a teacher base a lesson on a *mis*quotation of scripture. My favorite was in the mission field, when a zone leader said, "The Lord says that if ye are not one ye are not mine! Well, we're going to be number one in this mission!"

I remember coming home from church and telling my parents, "The teacher doesn't know anything, the kids wouldn't care if he did, and I don't want to go anymore." My parents' answer was always, "Well, if you can't learn, then you can help others learn."

The other stock answer is, "You don't go to meetings to partake, you also go to give."

I tested it. I started adding to the lessons by raising the questions that really mattered to me. Like, if governments are ordained of God and we're supposed to obey the law of the land, why can't Mormons accept welfare from that government? Now I know the answer — but the teacher didn't. He stumbled through a murky attempt at answering and then went on, leaving me unsatisfied and him feeling bad because his lesson had just been shattered.

Not only did the teachers hate me for my questions, they also got really sick of my corrections. But somehow I thought it would add to the lesson if the teacher didn't keep putting Jerusalem on the Jordan River right where Jericho is supposed to be. I believed that it was important to point out that it wasn't *all* dissenters who were condemned in the Book of Mormon — only the ones that turned traitor and defected to the enemy.

And so the teachers began to pray, I'm sure, for me to fall off a cliff just before Sunday School. Also the other kids. This is the biggest joke of all: "You can help the other kids learn." Garbage. The other kids resent having to sit and listen to the teacher. They *certainly* don't want some smartmouth fellowkid to try to "help" them learn.

And so all my attempts to follow my parents' advice ended up leaving the teachers antagonized, the other kids hostile, and me still just as bored by church and now a little frustrated by it as well.

And Scouting was the worst. I hate Scouting. I hate tents. I hate sleeping bags. I hate insects. I hate tying knots. The merit badges in the areas that interest me are so silly and superficial that they seemed to me to be a waste of time. And of course the merit badges in the areas that didn't interest me — well, they didn't interest me.

So at the age of thirteen I declared a one-boy boycott of MIA. I also avoided Sunday School as often as my conscience would let me (which was pretty often), and I attended only priesthood meeting and sacrament meeting regularly. After all, I told myself, those are the "commanded" meetings. The others are just auxiliaries.

Even though I was able to whip myself into shape to go on a mission, after my mission I found church even more boring, and very nearly left. Now I'm active — for the first time since childhood. But I'll tell you a secret: the lessons still bore me silly. The only thing I gain from meetings now is that I've committed enough sins for the calls to repentance to strike home.

What could my parents have done differently? I don't know. I don't think they could have done anything. I couldn't help the fact that I was more intelligent than average. The teachers couldn't very well prepare their lessons only for me — just because I knew the scriptures back and forth didn't mean that the rest of the class did, and they would have been lost. The Church is geared to reaching the majority, at least in the classes.

But here's the ironic thing. When I went inactive, when I was basically living a sinful life, *then* the machinery of the Church mobilized. Then they came home teaching to my door. Then they welcomed me effusively to church, made it a point to welcome me and invite me to the activities, gave me responsible callings so I would be sure to take part.

Where were all those things when I was a very bright boy who was vitally interested in the gospel but didn't find anyone in the Church organization who had time to deal with him on his level?

As long as I was an intelligent but law-abiding boy, people just wished I'd go away. Then I went away — and as a sinner, I fit right into the program.

Maybe if my parents had really talked to me about the important things in the gospel, it might have made a difference. Maybe if a home teacher had made it a point to discuss things on *my* level, instead of talking down. Maybe if a teacher had gone the extra mile and studied up a little extra, just to have something for *me*.

That sounds really selfish. And I really don't look at the Church as an organization that exists solely to serve *me*. But I'm not the only kid who was in that situation. And so I think I'm not the only kid who's going to be lost from the Church out of utter boredom. I came back. Will the others?

Arlene

I have always been active in the Church, I have attended meetings, taught classes, visiting taught, I have been everything I was supposed to be.

But the time when I realized that not only was the gospel true, but also it *mattered* that the gospel was true — the first time I really felt the Spirit move in my own life was when my father laid his hands on my head and gave me peace and confidence by the power of his priesthood.

God lives in your home when that home has a man who can act for God. I wish more men in the Church realized that when those hands rest on their children's heads, they are blessing them with more than just the words they say at that moment.

My father's hands on my head felt like eternity pressing down, reaching inside, and lifting me up and out of myself.

Reuben

My parents always made a real distinction between commandments and family rules. The family rules could be changed by Dad and Mom — exceptions could be made — and even though disobedience brought punishment, following the punishment came reasonably quick forgetting. It wasn't all that serious.

But the commandments of God — that was serious.

I remember the first time I ran afoul of the commandments. I was five years old and we were living in this crazy little village of old World War II surplus prefabricated houses. Almost like trailers. I guess it was just temporary housing for employees at the new factory where Dad worked. There were narrow streets and playgrounds on every block, and on every third or fourth corner there was a little store, kind of a quick-stop store, only back before those were known all over the place.

That store had a rack that was full of Twinkies, donuts, and my favorite thing in the whole world: Hostess cupcakes.

Money was pretty scarce for us then — I was sixth of seven, and Dad wasn't earning all that much. But for some reason or other — I think I got it from Grandpa and Grandma for my birthday — I got a whole dollar.

My parents saw this as a great time to teach me about tithing. So when I got the dollar, Dad was right there with ten dimes. He explained to me that the ten dimes were equal to the dollar, and so I consented to the trade — to me, ten dimes looked like a lot *more* than a dollar.

Then Dad explained that Heavenly Father gives us everything we have. Well, I'd have to take it on faith — to me, Grandpa gave me the dollar and Mom and Dad gave me everything else. But if Dad wanted to give the credit to Heavenly Father, fine with me.

And then Dad said, "And so we always give one-tenth of what we receive to the Church. This is called tithing. You've just received ten dimes. Out of ten dimes, how many does the Lord get?"

I wasn't too good at fractions when I was five. I pushed about half the dimes over toward Dad. He laughed. Then he held up just one of the dimes.

"This dime will go to the Lord. The other dimes you can spend. So you put this dime in your drawer, and on Sunday we'll take it to the bishop."

So I put the dime in the drawer and then sometime the next day or so Mom took me to a toy store and I squandered the ninety cents on some forgettable toy.

On Friday morning I put on my socks and discovered the dime. Ah ha! I picked it up and bounded out into the kitchen and said, "Mommy, look what I found."

Mommy had a good memory. "That's your tithing dime, put it back."

So I went back to the bedroom and put on my socks. And my shoes. And all the time I thought about how that dime was exactly what it cost to buy a package of Hostess cupcakes. With creamy centers. It's true — in those days they only cost a dime.

So I grabbed the dime, tucked it into a fist, and charged out of the house.

"What have you got in your hand?" Mother called after me.

"Nothing!" I yelled and I was out the door.

I bought the cupcakes.

Then I kind of hid them behind my back and walked on past our house on the way to kindergarten.

My older sister was out in front of the house. She went to the same school I went to.

"What do you got behind your back?" she asked me.

"Nothing," I said. After all, if the answer works once, maybe it'll work twice.

"I can see them, Rube," she said. "You spent your tithing dime, didn't you?"

Sisters are like that — always trying to be mothers. Right at the moment I really hated her. "No I didn't," I said.

"Sure," she said. "I'm going to tell Mom."

She headed back to the house. And so I took off toward school. I caught up with a group of my friends. And then, afraid of being caught with incriminating evidence, I gave them the cupcakes and ran on to school.

I had neither the dime nor the cupcakes.

And on the way home, the same sweet sister took me to the spot where I had given the cupcakes to my friends. There were the cupcakes in the grass beside the sidewalk, crushed and stamped on. Covered with ants.

"I don't care," I said.

"You're gonna," she said.

And then I got home. That night Dad took me into the kitchen and he and Mom sat down and I sat down and we had a long talk. No, I mean they had a long talk and I had a long listen.

Dad explained that because I wasn't eight yet, the Lord didn't hold me accountable for breaking his commandments.

"That means," he said, "that when you break the commandments now, Reuben, the Lord isn't going to punish you. He is
very sad, though, that you didn't care enough to keep his
commandment. You spent the ninety cents, and yet you
couldn't save ten cents for the Lord."

I felt pretty bad by then. Mostly because my parents were
upset at me, and even though it's easy for a little kid to ignore
the fact that his parents are going to be upset, it is impossible for
a little kid not to care when his parents *are* upset. You know?

And then Dad laid the big one: "The Lord isn't going to
punish you for this. However, Reuben, I am."

I didn't think this was fair. If the Lord was willing to let me
off, who was Dad to take matters into his own hands? Actually, I
didn't think this at the time. At the time I just knew that Dad
was pretty good at the laying on of hands — especially when the
backside was the target area.

"I'm going to punish you because if I punish you now, then
after you turn eight you'll remember to obey the Lord's commandments and then he won't punish you. I'm pretty sure
you'd rather be punished by me, now, than by the Lord, later."

This was a bad guess on his part. I would rather have been
boiled in oil later than punished by Dad then.

Anyway, Dad asked which I would rather have, a spanking
with his hand on my bare bottom, or a spanking with a ruler on
my pants. What a choice. But I was really a modest little kid and
I chose the ruler on the pants. It stung and I cried. I've never
missed a tithe. The Lord's had the whole 10 percent ever since.

Mostly because I remember how the things I bought with
my tithing money turned out getting mashed into the ground.
That meant a lot more than the spanking. Because even now,
when money gets kind of tight, I think of those cupcakes
covered with ants and I figure the Lord'll do a better job of
spending my tithing money than I would.

Cathy

Mom and Dad were good, church-going people. They loved to remind us kids of that. They were always telling us to be righteous and obey the commandments. And we had to sit still in church. We sat still because going out into the lobby meant a walloping. We were doggone reverent little kids.

But that didn't teach us respect for the Church. Because there was another lesson that I heard really loud, all week long. I heard about how the bishop's wife was a busybody who was trying to run the ward, and you'd better not tell the bishop anything because he told his wife and in three hours the entire ward knew.

I heard how the Sunday School superintendent had no idea of the right way to run a Sunday School. I heard them making fun of a sacrament meeting speaker's southern accent. I heard Dad say he didn't want to hear anything a certain General Authority had to say, because he was a Republican. I heard Mom complain about how the visiting teachers always came when she was busiest and then stayed forever and she just wished they'd stay away for a month so she could catch up.

I remember clearly my parents planning an evening out, and then remembering at the last minute that the ward teachers were coming. They went anyway, and told us kids to tell them that they forgot. We told them.

Mom and Dad always took us to church. We never shopped on Sunday, never even watched TV on the sabbath. They fulfilled all their callings. They constantly invoked the commandments.

In fact, that was one of the worst things about my teenage years. It was impossible for me just to make a mistake. No, if I did something that Mom and Dad didn't like, it wasn't just dumb or childish or something. It was always wicked.

"Would you want Jesus to see you in that dress?" Mom asked me. I remember when I was about seventeen and things were at their worst, she said that to me and I laughed at her. "How dare you laugh!" she said. But I just kept laughing. There she was in a housedress and shambly slippers with her hair up in curlers looking like five miles of bad road. I said, "Mother, you wouldn't want Jesus to see you right now either. And I don't think he *wants* to see us."

She slapped my face.

Somehow the Lord always seemed to be on my parents' side. No matter how rude or intolerant they were of my wishes, there was a commandment to back them up. "The idler will not eat the bread of the worker" was the reason they insisted I stay home from just about anything that sounded fun. I had to "help."

"Do unto others as you would have them do unto you" was the reason I had to give in to my brothers and sisters in every argument. I always wondered why *they* didn't ever have to do unto me the way they wanted me to do unto them.

"Honor thy father and thy mother" was the big one, though. That one I heard about eighteen times a day. No matter what I did that might flout their orders, I was dishonoring my father and my mother. In our last fight before I left home to marry before the pregnancy began to show, my mother screamed at me, "Honor thy father and thy mother that thy days may be long upon the land that the Lord thy God giveth thee!"

I screamed right back, "When God said that he was talking to the people who had honorable parents!"

Because of the way my parents used the Church as a weapon against me, I really came to think of the Church and the gospel as the enemy. It's funny. There's never been a time in my life when I would have said that I didn't think the gospel was true. I've always believed in the gospel. But I absolutely hated the Church. I guess because I always thought of the Church as being on my parents' side. And after all those years of hearing my parents criticize everything and everybody, I didn't exactly have this big reservoir of respect for the bishop and the leaders and the teacher or anybody. *Now* I know better. But I sure didn't learn it from my parents.

Todd

When I first started having responsibilities in the Church, Mom and Dad always treated my church duties as if they were exactly as important as theirs. If I had to collect fast offerings, that was exactly as important as Dad getting to high council meeting: and the cars and schedules were adjusted according-ly. If I had to give a talk in church, Dad would stay in our ward instead of going to the ward he was assigned to, and the whole family would be right there on the third row in the middle, listening. Afterward they would discuss what I said just as seriously as we discussed what Dad said in talks, or Mom.

The message came through loud and clear: whatever job you have in the Church, it's absolutely vital that you do it, do it well, and enjoy doing it.

And going to church — I remember it being absolutely boring in sacrament meeting when I was seven or eight or so. But then I began to notice that for a half hour or more after church, in the car on the way home and then sitting around the living room, everybody would be discussing the subject of the sacrament meeting talks. And if I didn't listen in sacrament meeting, I was completely left out of the discussion.

Those discussions were worth getting into. Dad never really spent much time repeating what the speaker had said. Instead he'd ask us questions about what next. I mean, if the speaker had talked about how we go about repenting, Dad would start talking about the Atonement, and how Christ saved us from our sins. Then he'd start asking questions. Not the silly kind of question you sometimes see in manuals, like, "Why is it impor-tant to repent?" but really meaningful questions — hard and personal questions — like, "Todd, have you ever felt like the Lord wasn't happy with you? Have you ever had a hard time praying?" And I'd say yes, maybe. And then he'd say, "Do you feel free to tell us about it?" It was perfectly all right to say no. But if I said yes, then I'd have to tell the story. And then Dad would ask someone else, "Why do you think Todd felt like he couldn't pray? Didn't he want to repent?" And so on and so on.

We always had discussions like that. Dad always took sacrament meeting talks and Sunday School lessons and made us think of what those ideas actually meant to us. Why did they matter? And if this was true, what about this? Really? And where do you get that idea from?

Seminary wasn't immune. I remember coming home from school full of ideas from the seminary class — we Mormons in my high school had been talking about the idea all day. It was kind of a far-out doctrine, completely new to me, but it sounded good. I came in and told Dad all about it.

He listened all the way through, asked a few clarifying questions, and then he said, "OK, now tell me where the Lord said that."

I didn't know.

"Look it up."

I said I'd rather not.

"Look, Todd," he said to me, "you're believing this as if it came straight from the prophet's lips. But you don't *know* whether the Lord taught that or not. Now you have a responsibility to find out."

So I studied the subject and reported to him that even though the idea was interesting, it really didn't jibe with the D&C. And then we spent an hour talking about what the D&C was talking about — by the way, the subject was intelligences and light and truth — and Dad was very thoughtful after we were through. He said, "Actually, son, I think your seminary teacher has a good point, even though there's a lot of implications he didn't go into." And then Dad smiled and said, "Keep reading and we'll talk sometime about those implications."

And Dad didn't forget. A week later he brought up the subject again, and I learned to really search the scriptures, really find out for myself.

And then Dad would always ask, "Have you prayed about that?" Whenever I made a decision, he'd ask, "Have you prayed about that?" If I couldn't answer yes, he wouldn't have much respect for my decision. Not that he didn't think I was smart enough to decide on my own sometimes; just that he thought anybody who didn't know enough to pray before deciding something just wasn't worth paying much attention to.

Once I said to him, "I prayed, Dad, but I just didn't get an answer."

He looked at me for a while and then he said, "Well, I guess the Lord trusts you enough to let you decide on your own." And that was that. He accepted my decision. As long as I had approached the Lord, the decision was worthy of respect. Of course, that wasn't about decisions like what color socks to wear. He used to say, "Anybody who asks the Lord whether to shave before he showers deserves not to get answers to his prayers. The Lord is busy and he expects us to make the routine decisions ourselves."

From Mom and Dad I learned that the gospel is the most exciting thing in the world, the Church the most important organization. I learned that because not only did they work hard and discuss things, but also they expected us kids to work at exactly the same level, discuss at the same level. What we were thinking, what we were doing about the Church and the gospel — they treated us as being exactly as important before the Lord as they were.

It was like my Mom once said to me: "Todd, sometimes I think you must have been older than me in the spirit world. You must have been my older brother. Because sometimes you're so wise, and I learn so much from you." That's really something, when your mother treats you with so much respect like that. I've always felt, all my life, that the Lord was really hoping

I'd make it to the celestial kingdom. That he was really on my side. I sure knew that my parents were.

LaDell

The Spirit of God lived at our house. I can't remember a time when I wasn't aware of my parents' testimony of the gospel.

It was the way Mom and Dad prayed — they just talked to God. For instance, when I was a little kid and Dad and Mom were struggling while Dad got his degree, sometimes they didn't know where the next meal was coming from. They didn't have vague family prayers about, "Bless us with the material things of life of which we stand in need." Instead we'd sit there for a few minutes before the family prayer and Dad and Mom would discuss the things we were going to pray about, so that we all understood, and would ask us if there was anything we needed help with. Then Dad or Mom — and as we kids grew older, we prayed, too — would offer the prayer.

So when there were financial problems, Dad might say, "Heavenly Father, right now we're completely out of food in the house except for soda crackers and a little milk. That's what we're going to have for breakfast. In order for us to get through the week until Mother's check comes, we need at least twenty dollars. We have done everything we know how to do in order to honestly get that money. We ask thy help in getting it."

And then that night there would be dinner on the table, and before dinner Dad would show us the envelope that the check had come in, or would tell us how one of his professors had said to him, "I know how tough it is for a student with a family. Do you happen to need anything for a while just to help get by?" And Dad would recognize the answer to prayer, and he would swallow his pride, and say, "If I had twenty dollars I could get through the week." And the professor said, "Is that all? Here. Pay me back when you can."

And then on nights like that we would say the blessing on the food and Mom would cry during the blessing, when we said,

"We thank thee for this food." Even now, when money isn't a problem, Mom or Dad will sometimes give the blessing on the food and say, "We have known how it feels to wonder where our next meal is coming from, and thou hast always blessed us in the past. We are truly grateful for our plenty." And then during dinner they sometimes retell those old stories to the younger kids who weren't alive when they happened. And also to remind us older kids of the Lord's blessings.

Spiritual things have always been taken so seriously. We have always talked about them openly, of course. But a special tone of voice is used. Mom gets soft and whispery, and Dad's voice deepens and he talks softer, too. Reverently. And the simple rituals of the gospel are treated carefully.

Like when I was about to prepare my portfolio for my scholarship application in art. I had all the stuff I had already done, but I was also going to do a painting especially for the application. I went to my father and told him that I was really afraid, and that I wanted to make sure that I chose the right subject for my painting and that I just didn't know if I could really do a good enough job. He just smiled and asked if I had prayed. I said yes. And then he said, "Would you like a blessing?" I said yes. In fact, that was what I had been hoping for.

So he called Mom in — he never did any priesthood ordinances in our home without Mother there. And he asked the other kids to please turn down the radios or the TV. He didn't explain why — but he asked them in his reverent voice, and they knew that something important was going on in the house, even though it was private.

And then, with the house quiet, Dad and Mom and I would go into their bedroom or my bedroom. This time we went into my room, and Dad put his hands on my head and blessed me with confidence in my abilities, and blessed me that the right choice for my subject would be obvious to me, and that I would do my best work.

I did. And I got the scholarship. But that's the best thing about it: it would never have occurred to me or Dad to ask the

Lord to give me the scholarship. We only asked the Lord to help me deserve it. That was the important thing — deserving, not winning.

Later on in a family home evening I told my brothers and sisters about the experience and bore my testimony that the Spirit of God worked through our father because of his worthiness and his priesthood. And would you believe it? Every single one of the kids had their own story to tell, their own personal testimonies of how Dad had used his priesthood to influence their lives.

And then Mom talked about how when I was born the doctors were sure that she would die, but that Father gave her a blessing right there in the hospital and promised her that it wasn't the will of the Lord that she would die, and she knew right then that she would live. And he promised her that she would bear many wonderful children, and she cried as she told us that his promise had been fulfilled.

Don't misunderstand — we didn't have miracles every day or anything. That was the only real healing, really dramatic thing that had happened in the family. But we never needed the big dramatic things. We had so many constant reminders. So many testimonies.

We lived knowing that at any moment we could call upon the Lord and he would be there, willing to help us achieve our righteous purposes.

Just to tell you how pervasive this was, I remember when I was sixteen and my youngest sister was only three. Mom and Dad were both gone on a trip or something, and I was tending the kids. Darla asked me to hear her prayers, because she was used to having somebody listen as she prayed. But she didn't need any help.

She just prayed as Mother and Father had taught her to pray. She told Heavenly Father that she had been bad that day because she had gotten mad at her brother but that she and Barry had made up and they were friends again. She asked

Heavenly Father to protect Mommy and Daddy and bring them home again.

And then she said, and I can remember every word, she said, "And Heavenly Father, we had the most beautiful sunset tonight. The sky was red all over. You should have seen it." And she closed her prayer and went to bed. I just sat there crying. My parents gave us a love for the Lord, taught us a close relationship with him, right from the beginning. That doesn't mean that we always obeyed all the commandments and always loved going to church. But it did mean that we always knew we *should* obey the commandments and that we *should* love going to church.

And most of all my parents taught me that Heavenly Father loves me, and they loved me so much that I knew what it felt like to be loved. I'm just so grateful that I know that the family will go on forever. This is so silly, for me to be crying right now. I just know that heaven will be good, if it's like my home.

Listen, Mom and Dad:

1. Live the gospel.

2. Respect and honor the Lord and the Church, so that we never learn disrespect from you.

3. Share spiritual experiences with us. Let us know your testimonies. Let the Spirit of God live with us at home.

4. Teach us to pray with meaning.

5. Don't ever let us feel that the Church and the gospel are our enemy. We must be taught that the Lord has no tolerance for sin: but we must also learn that the Lord has unending forgiveness for the sinner who repents.

6. Make the gospel an important part of our daily lives, a good and pleasant part, not just a Sunday duty, an interminable string of meetings.

7. And if one of us finds that our needs are not met by the Church, try to find a way to meet those needs yourselves. The Church can't do everything for us: you can fill in the missing places. In fact, it's your responsibility *first*.

8. Remember that activity in the Church doesn't mean perfect attendance at meetings. The meetings are where the Saints *prepare* to be active. It is at home, at work, in the neighborhood, in the school — that is where we are active in the Church.

Listen, Mom and Dad . . .

8
about
my
friends . . .

He may look long-haired and dirty and ugly to you, but to your son or daughter who brought him home, he's handsome and clever and exciting and maybe even kind.

She may wear too much makeup or use bad language or hang around with the wrong crowd, but she's a good friend to your son or daughter who brought her home — at least *they* think so.

Your children, once they start going to school, will start making friends, spending time with them, caring how they think and what they do and wanting to think and do likewise. They may choose good friends (in your opinion) or bad friends (in your opinion), but whatever your opinion, they are *friends*.

You want them to learn to be loyal, don't you? You want them to be open, trusting, sharing, loving people, don't you? Ah — but *you* know, and they don't, that it's possible to be loyal to the wrong people. You want to spare them some heartbreaking experiences.

There are ways you can still influence them, and you should do it — you don't walk away from a drowning man because he didn't ask for your help. But don't ever, ever make your children choose between their friends and you.

Because whichever way they end up choosing, it'll be a long time before they forgive you for making them choose.

Todd

For about two years, we lived in a town that was about half Mormon and half non-Mormon. The Church's influence was very strong. And it was possible for people to have all their friends be Mormon.

However, for some reason — actually, the reasons were many and strong — my closest friend at this time was Sam Polk, who wasn't Mormon. I think he was Baptist. We became friends because we were in the same P.E. class and we both hated football. Which is as good a reason as any to start a friendship.

But we *stayed* friends because I liked Sam, everything about him. He never said the kind of things that all my Mormon friends said. I mean, he reacted differently to the world, and yet his way of reacting was still a good way. He was talented and creative and exciting. He played the piano beautifully and wrote music that was sparse and lovely. He never did anything flashy just for show — he never bragged, never even talked about himself much.

Except to me.

Why?

One thing he told me once was kind of a clue. After school one day he came over to my house with me, partly because my house was close to the school and partly because we had a pretty nice piano (an old upright, but it was in tune) and the crummy little spinet at his house sounded like a five-dollar toy piano. He sat down at the piano and as he talked to me he just let his fingers wander, just touched keys here and there. I really wasn't aware of the sound, because I was listening to his words.

I don't remember what he said, but I do remember that he was sad — there were some family problems. The music fit his mood. Slow, soft, and a little discordant.

Anyway, all of a sudden we both realized that my Mom was standing in the room. We stopped the conversation, Sam stopped playing, and we turned and looked at her. Both of us, I guess, were wondering how much of the conversation she had heard, because our faces looked embarrassed — and so did hers.

"I'm sorry," she said. "I couldn't hear what you were saying, don't worry."

And then there was a silence, or else I said something like, "That's OK," but anyway, there was a hole in the conversation, and all of a sudden Mom walked right in and put her arms around Sam. Just hugged him.

"Sam," she said, "your music is so beautiful and sad, it breaks my heart." If I had said that it would have sounded sarcastic, but Mom can say things like that so you know she means them from her soul.

Then, after giving him a little squeeze, she just left the room.

And Sam was sitting there crying. Well, not crying, exactly, but there were tears on his cheeks and he wasn't talking. He just kind of touched some keys on the piano, and then he turned to me and said, "I better go home now."

"Hey, you're not mad, are you?" I asked, because I was afraid that my mother might have offended him.

"No," he said. Then when he was out getting on his bike — and I remember there was a wind coming up, and our hair was blowing, and there was dust in the air — he smiled at me and he said, "Lucky you."

"How come?" I asked.

"Your Mom isn't a Mormon, Todd. She's a Christian." And then he rode off.

I didn't really get that, except as maybe kind of a joke, until the next year, when we were old enough to drive — and when the girls our age were able (at last) to date. Sam got a crush on Sally Brinton, who was the daughter of a bishop from another part of town. They talked a lot, he carried her books between classes, that kind of thing. And he talked to me a lot about what a great girl she was and how she was the only girl he had ever known that he could talk to almost the way he talked to me.

Sam wasn't exactly the socialite kind of guy. He was, to put it bluntly, shy. It took him four months to work up the courage to ask her out to a school dance.

The night he asked her he called me up before and talked for fifteen minutes to get his courage up.

Then, about an hour later, I called him to see how it went. He wouldn't talk to me.

The next day at school I asked him what happened. He apologized for not talking to me the night before. "I guess last night I hated all Mormons."

I asked why.

"She can't go out with me."

"Why not?" But I already knew why not.

"Because I'm not a Latter-day Saint. They're afraid that at the ripe old age of sixteen I might marry their daughter and carry her off to live with me in sin." He was really bitter.

What could I say? I knew that Mormon girls were counseled not to date non-Mormon guys, and I knew why, and I even agreed — in general. But Sam Polk! I didn't know a Mormon who was any kinder, any cleaner, any more righteous than my friend Sam.

Sam got over it, of course, but he never asked out any Mormon girls after that. And then we moved away after that school year.

The thing that made me connect this with what Sam had said about my mother is that I realized my Mom and Dad would never have just given a flat *no* about dating somebody just because he or she was non-Mormon. They would have advised against it in general, but they just didn't make quick judgments of our friends.

Like, I had a friend in college who wore his hair down to his shoulders and dressed like an absolute slob. He was Mormon, but not very actively so. There are some parents who might have hit the roof if their kid came home with a creepy looking friend like that. But my folks just asked me about him later, found out how I felt about the guy, that kind of thing. I made it clear I had no intention of dressing like him, and they just laughed, saying I'd look pretty silly with long hair like that, I didn't have a mean enough face.

"George doesn't have a mean enough face, either," my dad said. "He seems like a really nice guy."

So they never complained about the time I spent with George. And so George came over to our house a lot, and his hair started getting shorter and shorter until one day it was as short as mine and he was able to come and tell us about his mission call — the jerk got his three days before I got mine. I was really jealous!

If my parents had refused to let me associate with him just because he "looked like a hippy" then he would never have had the influence of my family and maybe he would never have gone on a mission. And I've seen it happen so often in other families: parents who forbid their kids to associate with somebody who looks sleazy end up losing their kid, not keeping him.

That's what I meant about Sam. My mom and dad accepted him, just as I did, for the wonderful person he was. They *knew* him, and because they took the time to understand him, my friendship with Sam didn't take me away from my family — it brought me even closer.

My folks have been that way all my life. They just don't prejudge my friends. I guess they always figured — my mother even said it once — "If Todd has found something to like about him, then there's something to like about him." Right on, folks!

Arlene

During all my grade school, before junior high, we lived in California and I went to the public schools. Of course there were several black students in my classes, and always a lot of Chicanos. One of my best girlfriends was Rita Morales, and Todd McGregor hung around our group, and nobody ever even commented on the fact that Todd McGregor was black and Rita was Mexican and her parents spoke Spanish. We didn't ignore it, either — I mean, Rita sometimes spun off a long string of Spanish when she was angry, and we weren't blind, we could see the different colors. We just didn't care.

And then we moved to a city that was 99 percent Mormon. It was my first year in junior high school. It was hard for me to adjust to the change because I'd grown up all in one neighborhood and I didn't know anybody in the new school; but they all knew each other.

After a few weeks, though, I began to at least be talked to, and I thought I might actually like school a little. And maybe even make friends. One day a group of girls even asked me to walk home with them.

On the way home, though, they started telling jokes. And all of the jokes — I mean all of them — were about how dumb Negroes are, and they were terrible, I still don't see that they were at all funny, but the girls just laughed and laughed at them. Finally I spoke up — I was really angry — and I asked if any of them had ever known a Negro. None of them had, and one of them said, laughing, "I once bumped into one on the street, but I went home and took a bath." They thought this was really hilarious.

But I just blew up. I yelled at them and told them that I had known a lot of Negroes and every one of them was nicer and cleaner and smarter than those girls — which wasn't strictly true, I think the average was about the same, but I was too mad to be logical. And finally I ran off in tears.

They laughed really loud as I ran away.

When I got home I was still crying and I told my mother what had happened. I kept saying that I hated those girls, they were awful, how could they say such things, on and on.

Finally I calmed down and my mother dried my eyes with her handkerchief (Mother always had a handkerchief) and she explained to me, she said, "The only reason those girls talked like that is because they've never even known a Negro, there aren't any at all in this town. They've heard grown-ups or older children tell these jokes, and they don't know any better. That's no reason to hate them. They're just ignorant; you were lucky enough to have more experience than they were."

"I still hate them," I said. "How can they judge people they don't even know."

"Just the way you're doing," Mom said to me. "You don't know those girls, either, and here you are telling me you hate them. You're being prejudiced, deciding because of one little incident that these girls are people you aren't going to like."

I still hated them.

But a few years later, when I grew up a little more, I finally learned the kind of tolerance that my mother was trying to teach me. Not that she always had that kind of tolerance herself, of course. But she taught me that I shouldn't even be intolerant of the bigoted and ignorant. Which is a lesson I've *tried* to observe all my life. Haven't always succeeded, of course!

Cathy

My parents and my friends? Ha. The Nazis versus the Communists.

No joke, that's what they called each other. My friends were always called "weirdos" and "beatniks" and "strange people" by my parents ("What kind of strange people are you hanging around with *tonight,* Cathy?"), and my Dad actually did call one of my boyfriends a Communist because he laughed at Dad's brand new Chevrolet as another example of materialism.

And my friends always called my parents The Nazis. This was because they were always checking on me. Especially when I was fourteen or so and my friends and I were just beginning to wear shorter skirts and makeup and the guys were growing Beatle-style or surfer-style hair — nowadays we call styles of that time "conservative," but in those days they were really radical. When I had friends over to the house, my parents would keep checking on us. We'd be sitting around talking or something, looking at magazines, and all of a sudden there'd be Dad.

"What kind of trash are you reading?" He never once waited until he saw the cover of the magazine or anything. He just assumed that if my friends and I were reading it, it would be trash. Once it was even the *Saturday Evening Post,* for goodness' sake. I showed him the cover and glared at him, but do you think he'd apologize? Not a chance. He just said, "Better watch it." Better watch what? I'm supposed to not read?

It was worse when I had a boyfriend over. Then we'd look up and there'd be these eyes watching us. We didn't dare sit on the same sofa, it was so bad.

I suppose my folks thought they were "protecting me."

All that they succeeded in doing was drive me away from home. I know, that sounds really melodramatic and everything, but you just get fed up with having your parents *humiliate* you in front of your friends. I learned really fast never to bring a boyfriend home, never to bring a girlfriend home, because my parents the Nazis would come down like the SS and check on us constantly.

And besides, my friends liked me. And I didn't think my parents did. In fact, I knew darn well they didn't. And let's face it. It's only human nature to prefer being with the people who like you.

LaDell

I think the biggest lesson I ever learned about friendship wasn't even taught to me by my parents. They didn't even know I learned it until I told them about ten years later.

When I was in second grade we were on double sessions or something because my school let out at noon. Mother was teaching at a private nursery school/kindergarten until two o'clock in the afternoon, while Dad was at the college every day working on his Ph.D. So in order that I wouldn't come home to an empty house, Mom and Dad made arrangements for me to get off the bus one stop before, with my friend Joey, and we would have lunch with his mother and she would tend me until my mom came home after work and picked me up. The younger kids were with Mom, of course, attending nursery school and kindergarten.

One day a girlfriend of mine — I can't remember her name — invited me to come to her house after school. I wanted to go, it sounded like fun. Her bus stop was the one *after* my house. I knew that if I asked anybody they'd tell me no. So I didn't ask. When the bus stopped at Joey's bus stop and Joey got out, I scrunched down in my seat so he wouldn't see me.

Then I went on to my girlfriend's house and we played until about three o'clock or so. Then I walked home.

When I got home Mom was like a crazy person, she had been so afraid I had been kidnapped or something she just grabbed me and cried and then she said, "Where were you! I've been worried sick!" and she told me how the school told her that I had definitely been there and Joey's mother had called and said, "Where's LaDell, she didn't get off the bus with Joey, he looked for her but she wasn't there." It was awful.

I knew that if I told the truth I'd really get in trouble.

So I did the obvious thing. I told a lie.

I said that Joey had been really mean to me all day, especially on the bus, that he had said bad things to me and I didn't want to be with him anymore, and so my girlfriend had told me I could stay with her and *her* mother would tend me, and that was why I had gone on to my girlfriend's house.

It was a complete lie. Joey was probably the sweetest, meekest little boy who ever lived and I can't imagine him being rude to anyone, or even getting mad.

But my lie achieved its purpose. Mom wasn't mad at me anymore. She was, however, a little perturbed at Joey. She called Joey's mother and told her she could stop worrying, I hadn't been run over by a truck. And then she told her about Joey being mean to me.

So that night about eight o'clock Joey called me. His mother was probably standing right there by him, and my mother was certainly standing by me.

"LaDell?" he asked.

"Yeah," I said.

"I'm really sorry I talked mean to you and made you feel bad." He really sounded like he meant it. Maybe he even believed that he had somehow made me angry. But I knew that he hadn't done anything to be sorry about at all. And yet my mother was listening. So I just said, "Oh, that's all right, Joey."

How kind of me, to forgive him for something he didn't even do!

Needless to say, Joey and I weren't friends after that. Not because Joey refused to have anything to do with me. No, we stopped being friends because I felt so awfully guilty whenever I saw him. I never have been able to cope with guilt.

Now you know that deep down inside me I'm really a rotten selfish little girl. No, I'm just joking.

Ha. Maybe I'm not!

Dave

I couldn't have lived without my friends when I was in high school. That sounds really dramatic, but it's true. I didn't have many friends, just two or three. But if I hadn't had them to lean on, them to care about me and listen to me, I would have gone crazy. I was so lonely at home.

I don't think my parents can help it. They just thought of me as a kid. I couldn't get anybody to take me seriously. My friends did. That's all. They just treated me like I was real.

It's a good thing my parents never hassled me about my choice of friends. Maybe they knew instinctively or something that even my weird friends were better than nothing. But actually, I don't think they even noticed whether I had friends or not. That sounds cynical, but my parents weren't great noticers.

My friends taught me about love and trust and dependability by being kind and trustworthy and dependable. They needed me — my parents didn't. I needed them, because my parents just didn't notice my needs. That's how simple it was. My parents weren't rotten or cruel or anything. Just not there. And my friends *were* there.

Listen, Mom and Dad:

1. If we like them, then there's something likeable about them.

2. If there's a danger, warn us about the danger — don't try to keep us from associating with our friends. That will only make us try to get closer to them — and further from you.

3. Don't judge them until you know them.

4. When we don't get along with our friends, don't immediately assume that we're right and our friends are wrong — help us learn *how* to be good friends.

5. Sometimes those friends of ours can give us things you aren't equipped to give: you aren't perfect, and maybe we will choose friends who will fill up the places in our lives where you have unintentionally left holes.

6. And please don't be jealous of our friends. Friends have things in common that parents and children just can't share. But if we learn how to love our friends, we'll be better equipped to love our families, too, in the long run.

9
I couldn't help turning thirteen

It's like falling off a cliff. You don't know which way is up. Suddenly when people say "teenagers" they mean you. They expect you to act like an adult (can't you stop acting like such a *child?*) but they expect you to obey like a child (you're not old enough to go off and do things like that alone!). You want to reach out and grab freedom because for the first time in your life you can see that it's within reach. But your parents — aha! For every ounce of freedom you can snatch, they try to pile on a pound of responsibility.

Parents, just because we're still not grown up doesn't mean that we can't handle some responsibility. But then, don't be fooled, either: we are still children, in many respects, however much we insist to the contrary. We still need you: we're too big to be kept in the barn, but make sure the corral fence is tall enough to keep us safe!

Dave

About the time I turned thirteen I became a one-man rhythm band. I couldn't help it. Every time I had to sit still for a few minutes, I couldn't stand it. I'd start tapping my feet or drumming my fingers or making weird noises in my throat or something.

I did it at dinner. All of a sudden I'd take my knife and start tapping things — the glasses, the butter dish, the casserole, the plates, making every single possible noise. My parents actually became impatient. Which was unusual for them. They complained. They mentioned the fact that the stereo was playing and I wasn't in rhythm. They suggested that other people might enjoy sacrament meeting more if I refrained from drumming on the bench. They even pointed out that they were about to go crazy from the strange noises I made in my throat.

Sometimes I stood at the bottom of the stairs and bellowed at the top of my lungs as long and as loud as I could.

The windows would shake. Mother would ask if I was all right.

Why did I do these things? I don't know. I didn't know at the time. All I know is that they made me very unpopular at my house.

This went on for at least a year. Then it stopped. I know it stopped because I don't do those things anymore. But I really don't know why or when I quit any more than I know why or when exactly I started.

I was just thirteen. And after a while I turned fourteen. I guess it's as simple as that. And, fortunately, my parents didn't throw me out of the house during that time. Though I'm sure there were many times they were tempted.

LaDell

Of course when I was about thirteen or so I started having special requirements, like darts in my blouses. I became clothes hungry, you know? I read *Seventeen* magazine for the fashions and *Sixteen* magazine for the movie stars and the rock singers. And every time I saw a new fashion or heard of a new record or a new movie I asked my parents for money.

I was very direct. I have to laugh about it now. I had no subtlety. I'd just walk up to Mom or Dad and say, "Mo-om," or "Da-ad" — whenever I wanted something *mom* and *dad* became whiny, two-syllable words. Immediately they knew I was going to ask for money. Immediately they got set for the ordeal of saying no.

And I made it an ordeal for them. I never forgot. If I wanted a sweater, I would keep bringing it up. "If I had that sweater, I wouldn't be freezing *cold* right now." And Dad would answer, "If you can get a sheep to donate the wool, you have my permission to knit yourself a sweater."

Mom would come home with the groceries and I'd say, "If you hadn't bought any of that dumb macaroni, you probably could have bought me my sweater." To which she would reply, "If I let you starve to death you wouldn't want a sweater any more." To which I would reply, "If you let me freeze to death I won't want the dumb macaroni, either."

That could go on all winter. I don't know how my parents stood it. Sometimes they didn't. I remember one night when I had nagged about the money to buy a Beatles album for the umpty-fourth time, Dad slammed his pen down on the table and said, really slowly and really softly, "For every time in the next four hours that I hear any reference to money, the Beatles, or records, or anything like unto it (Dad gets biblical when he's angry) my daughter LaDell is going to lose the privilege of using the stereo for a week."

I was so stubborn that by the time the night was over, I had lost the use of the stereo for a month and a half. And Dad stuck to it, too.

Eventually I learned to be more subtle, and finally I grew up enough to learn how hard it is to earn money and how many directions the money has to go. But oh, the agony my parents went through until I learned it!

Todd

When I got into junior high school I felt like I wasn't a child anymore. True, I wasn't much over five feet tall at the time, and I still had to ride a bicycle to get from one place to another (or persuade a parent to let me hitch a ride with them) and I still had to go to school every day and actually, when you get right down to it, not that much had changed. But I felt like I wasn't a child, and so I insisted that I not be treated like one.

My parents really tried to respect my desires at that time, too. They still insisted on some basic family rules — like, if I wasn't going to be home at the usual time I should call and let them know where I was and when I'd be home. Also, I was given strict limitations on where I should *not* go — for example, to the swimming pool without prior clearance from my parents; to the shopping mall unless I had already cleared in advance what I was going to buy; or across the main highway, since they didn't want to have to worry about me handling my bike in the heavy traffic.

Of course, I felt like these were little-kid restrictions and it just wasn't fair for them to keep me tied down like that. After all, I was in *seventh grade.*

But one time something happened that changed both their attitude and mine. I had permission to go to the shopping mall with my friend Rodney. Rodney was going to buy something, but I was not to take any money with me except for five cents for a treat. In those days five cents could buy a treat.

So Rodney and I bicycled over to the mall and locked our bikes to the rack and went wandering around inside looking at things. After a little while Rodney and I separated, he to go to the sporting goods store, I to keep looking around at the plastic models in the hobby store. Coveting.

After a little while, though, Rodney came walking really quickly into the hobby store. His face looked completely white, and he just seemed scared. I asked him what was wrong. He told me that this really mean-looking grownup man had followed him into the restroom and kept trying to touch him. Rodney had told him to cut it out, but the guy had kept grabbing at him. Rodney had finally pulled away and run out of the bathroom. "But he's still following me around."

He pointed out the guy. He was standing outside the hobby store, innocently watching the electric trains through the window.

"Maybe he just likes electric trains," I said.

"He followed me," Rodney insisted.

So we waited around in the store for a while, and then we decided to see if he was really following Rodney. By this time the guy had moved away from the trains. Maybe he was gone.

But the minute we got outside the store into the mall, there he was. He kept about fifteen feet behind us. He wasn't trying to make any secret out of the fact that he was following. He kept watching us — both me and Rodney. By then we were really scared. We kept telling each other that he wouldn't try anything with both of us there, but we didn't believe it. After all, he was *following* both of us.

Our first impulse, of course, was to get out of there — get out on our bicycles and ride away.

We were almost at the door when I stopped Rodney and whispered, "This is stupid. Once we're away from the people in the mall we won't be able to call for help."

Rodney still wanted to leave, but I wouldn't go, and I wouldn't let him go, either. Besides, he wasn't too anxious to go *anywhere* alone right at that moment. So we kept wandering around the mall. Finally I saw a sign that said Security, and I realized that there were always policemen or at least guards in the mall.

But Rodney didn't want to go to them. "I don't want to tell them about it," he said, and I could see why, I mean, he had almost died of embarrassment telling *me* what the guy had tried to do. But finally we agreed that it was the only way we could be safe. So we went in and told them.

It turned out that the mall security force had been trying to find a way to get that guy out of the mall for weeks — they were sure he was up to something, but nobody had complained. They immediately hauled him in (they were careful not to let him see us, though), Rodney identified him. They called our parents and they came down. The guy confessed right away, though, and so all Rodney had to do was sign a statement. We didn't go to court or anything.

Anyway, when Mom and Dad got me home, Mother was really upset. She kept saying, "It makes me *ill* to think that there are people like that in the world." And finally she said, "Well, one thing's for sure, I'm definitely not letting Todd out of my sight again."

That was the worst thing I had heard all day. "That isn't fair," I said, "I didn't do anything!"

But she was too upset to listen to reason right then. She just kept saying, "When I think of what might have happened to you."

But later on that night she had calmed down, and Dad commented, "But it *didn't* happen, and the reason it didn't happen was because Todd thought quickly and did exactly the right thing. He might have lost his head, but he didn't." And then after discussing it for a while, Mom and Dad decided that I had proved that I was mature enough to be trusted, and the rules were relaxed a little, instead of being tightened, which had been Mom's first impulse.

But the funny thing was, while Mom and Dad had learned that I was growing up, *I* had learned that I wasn't as grown up as I thought. I can still remember how glad I was when Mom and Dad walked into the security office there in the mall. All I wanted right then was for them to grab onto me and take me out of there and away from all the sleazy people in the world. You know the feeling?

So they relaxed the rules a little, and at the same time I decided I didn't mind the rules so much anymore. All in all, a good compromise, I think.

What really scares me, though, is to think of what might have happened if I really *hadn't* been mature enough to cope with the situation. What if Rodney and I had left the mall and tried to go home on our bicycles? Maybe nothing would have happened. But maybe something really terrible could have happened. My parents were *already* trusting me a great deal. It makes me really scared now, looking at my little girl who isn't even walking yet, to realize that someday I'm going to have to let her out into the world — she's going to *insist* on being on her own. What if she isn't ready? And yet it would be cruel if I kept her so locked up that she never learned how to take care of herself. It's such a narrow line to walk.

Listen, Mom and Dad:

1. No matter how annoying we are, endure! We *will* grow out of it.

2. And no matter how young we still seem to you, we *are* growing up. Give us a chance to prove it. But — not *too* much responsibility all at once. Because we still need to be guided and protected, even though we hate to admit it.

Listen, Mom and Dad...

10
what you
taught me
about sex

It's true. The kids will find out about the birds and bees —
somehow. For them to learn the facts, you don't ever need to
talk to your children about sex. In fact, even those of you who *do*
talk to your children about it probably wait to do so until years
after they first found out the information.

But the facts aren't always the truth! The way *you* tell it and
the way they hear it from someone else — that makes all the
difference in the world.

Todd

My mother taught me the truth about sex. I don't mean she
sat me down to talk about the birds and the bees — I really can't
remember anybody actually doing that. When I was about nine
my parents left a cute little picture book lying around the house
that gave the basics — that was safe enough, since my little
brother didn't read yet, and my older brothers knew. After I'd
had plenty of time to read it, it suddenly disappeared.

There were a lot of blanks. But believe me, they got filled in
at school. I heard about *every* version of sex that could be
imagined. There's one type of pornography *nobody's* going to

be able to control: playground pornography. Half the "jokes" I didn't even understand for years.

But between the little book my parents left around and the whispers around the fences of the schoolyard, I knew the facts. But the facts aren't the truth. And my wife and I are both grateful that my mother dared to tell me the truth.

She didn't do anything formal, though. I mean, no "I have something I want to discuss with you, dear." Just in the course of conversation at one time, discussing a girl I liked, I think, she just casually said, "I hope when you turn sixteen and start dating that you don't feel like you have to go off in a car somewhere to have privacy with a girlfriend."

I told her I really wasn't worried about girlfriends. I think I was thirteen at the time.

"Just in case, though, so you know," she said. "When you really like somebody — not just every girl you date, of course — you'll want to have a chance to be alone, to put your arms around each other, kiss each other — now don't laugh, you *will*. I just don't want you driving off to some lonely road somewhere, or going to a drive-in movie. That makes it all seem so dirty. You just come home. I'll see to it that the living room is all yours. Nobody's going to peek or pry or wonder what's going on. You and your girlfriend can talk and express affection for each other right here at home."

I didn't really understand then how important this was, until I really did want privacy. Do you know how much privacy there is at college, when you have roommates, she has roommates, and neither of you has a car? I really came to appreciate my parents' living room. And she kept her word — never a single interruption, never a prying question.

I won't say I've never been tempted to go further with a girl than I ought to. But there in the family's living room it was easier to say no to temptation.

That wasn't all my mom taught me, though. When I was — I don't know, I guess sixteen or seventeen — she was talking to me again, who knows what about, but it just kind of came into the conversation. By then she was pretty sure I knew about sex — I'd have to be deaf and blind and kind of stupid not to, by then. And so she told me, "Your father and I have had our differences over the years, but I want to tell you something and I hope your wife will someday be able to say the same thing about you. Your father and I have always had a beautiful sexual relationship."

Let's face it. Mom and I had good communication, but I almost dropped dead on the spot. But she was so natural about it, and she didn't expect me to answer, so I just kind of swallowed and kept on listening.

"There are men who treat their wives as if they owned them, just using them until they're satisfied. But your father has always been gentle with me. He's always been very careful to make sure that I got as much enjoyment out of our lovemaking as he did — maybe more. When he makes love to me, I know he *loves* me. And if you can tell your wife that when you're making love, sex will always be a beautiful thing that will help tie the two of you together eternally."

Let me tell you. With just that one conversation, Mother undid all the ideas I had gotten from the guys at school. She taught me that sex *wasn't* what happened when you and a girl both lusted at the same time.

And I really believe my wife can say the same thing. I've never made love to her that I haven't been concentrating on helping *her* receive pleasure. It's a beautiful thing. And that's the truth about sex.

LaDell

It was funny — my parents really tried to tell me the facts of life. And I don't think I was particularly stupid, either. Mother took me aside one day and told me about the monthly period that would begin and what it meant and what sex was and how I was supposed to take care of my female problems, and that was it. I mean, there I was with the whole thing dumped on me — and I was supposed to memorize it all, I guess.

Mother had been very careful. I'm sure she worked hard at figuring out how to tell me (I'm the oldest in the family) and when she was through she probably breathed a sigh of relief. But I didn't.

She made such a big thing about it. It felt like she was saying, "Here it is. Look at it. Memorize it." And then the subject was closed.

So I worried about it. I had a lot of questions. I was worried. There was so much I didn't understand, you know? And yet I knew she thought she had done a good job of telling me — I didn't want to go to her and say, "Hey, you failed at teaching your daughter about sex."

Finally one day I screwed up my courage and went in and asked. I was so uptight I *cried*, which was silly. I was right — she was hurt that I hadn't understood the first time. But she went through the whole discussion again, which cleared up some of the questions, but there were others that I was really afraid to ask, and she looked like she just wanted to get the whole thing over with.

It wasn't until I got into some child development classes at the university that I began to get the answers. And that's a long time to wait!

About a month and a half before I got married, my fiance and I were talking. And I told him about this. We had been talking, I think, about how we were going to handle teaching *our* children about sex. For him, there had never been any questions or problems. His parents had both sat down with him when he was a kid, maybe ten or eleven, and explained the whole thing, very naturally, and then kept the subject open for quite a while in case he had any questions. We agreed — that's how we want to handle it with our kids!

It was that night, talking with my husband-to-be, that I found out the answers to my last questions. I asked him what happened to the *man,* I mean physiologically as well as psychologically. And he told me openly, though it wasn't really all that easy (How do you talk about sex to the person you're going to be doing it with in just a few months without feeling a *little* awkward?), and I finally felt at ease about it.

I just wish my parents had saved me all those years of worry by letting me feel natural about discussing it with them back when I was a little kid!

Reuben

OK, Mom and Dad and the bishop and everybody else told us we weren't supposed to go to bed with girls until we were married. Fine. The problem came with all the *other* stuff. The stuff they don't tell you about, like masturbation — it's still hard to discuss, you know? If somebody had talked so I could under- stand, it would've saved some grief. I'm sorry, but when the bishop called me in for my first interview, I hadn't reached puberty, *I* didn't know what masturbation was. And the bishop, he says, "Reuben, do you mastervate?" I mean, he pronounced it like it was spelled with a *v.* I'd never heard the word before, but I sure knew it was dirty from the way he asked it.

He said, "Do you know what that means?" and I said no, so then he gave me just about the world's worst definition. For years I had no idea what the word *mastervation* meant — let alone how to spell it!

I've figured out since then that the bishop was probably as embarrassed as I was. He was trying to get through a tough interview as fast and painless as he could. So he didn't check to see if I *understood.*

I didn't.

I had been masturbating for a couple of years before I finally made the connection. The dictionary — when I finally found out the right spelling and looked it up — just said, "self-abuse." That's a big help: I didn't kick myself in the shins or jump off tall buildings, I figured I wasn't abusing myself, therefore I wasn't masturbating. Now, I wasn't so dumb I didn't know I was doing something *wrong* — I just didn't think it was *seriously* wrong. It wasn't until I was sixteen in a bishop's interview when all of a sudden it hit me like a bolt of lightning that what I was doing and what he was asking about were the same thing!

Well, by then it was a habit, complete with fantasizing and everything, and I really had a problem. I know it sounds kind of sick, but that's the way it gets: I looked forward every day to that time.

Nobody knew what was going on. My parents never suspected.

I really fought that problem. I thought I had it licked before I went into the mission field, but sometimes you get so down, so depressed, that it's like taking a drug, it makes you forget, it makes you feel so good for a little while. Afterwards, of course, once you know it's a sin, then you feel even worse, you feel awful. But you just can't stop.

It takes a heck of a lot more willpower than going on a diet.

And then there's the other thing. They ask you, "Do you masturbate?" as if they were asking you, "Did you murder your mother?" You think that if you say yes they're going to excommunicate you or something. I remember one time in priests quorum this guy came in to talk about sex — every now and then they have some guy come in and talk about sex, but he always talks as if none of us knew what sex was, which we've all known since we were old enough to hear a dirty joke, so nobody listens — but the guy said, "Masturbation is a serious sin. You could be excommunicated for masturbation!"

Well, right then and there I decided that never never never was I going to tell the bishop about my masturbating problem. The guy probably meant well, I mean, you know, he probably figured that if he scared us bad enough we'd stop or not do it. But what about me? I really needed *help* to stop, but no way was I going to go in and tell the bishop and get *excommunicated*. I figured I'd just repent between me and the Lord.

Well, finally I found out that unless you really are defiant about it or something, nobody's going to excommunicate you or anything. But by then I was twenty-three. And finally I could ask for some help to get over the problem. I won't say I didn't fall sometimes after that, but when you know the bishop is on your side, when you know you're not the only guy in the world who does it, it really helps, you know?

If I could tell my parents anything about sex, I'd tell my dad to come to his kids and say, "Look, kid, one of the things about sex is that you can do it to yourself. You probably call it by some other name, if you know about it, but the real name for it is masturbation. If you do it or if you've already done it, you won't go blind and your ears won't fall off and you won't get excommunicated. But it can become a lousy habit that messes up your whole life. And when you're doing that, the Lord just can't get through to you as well. The Lord gave you sex organs so that you and a wife could bring forth children into a happy marriage, not for you to play around with. It's *wrong* to masturbate. But if you have already done it, don't die over it. Just tell me, I know how it is, you think I wasn't a kid?" But then, I think my dad would've died before he'd ever have admitted to me that he ever did anything like that. Maybe he didn't. But he could have *helped* me by talking to me about it, telling me that I wasn't a permanent pervert. That normal people sometimes did it, but they shouldn't.

When I get married and have kids, I'm going to make sure they can talk to me about sex and about the real problems they have with it. If my kid's got a problem, I want him to know he can tell me about it.

Arlene

I'd really rather not talk about that. Is that all right? It's just not something that I've ever discussed or that I like to discuss, and I don't want to be quoted about it or anything. Don't worry — I'm one of those good girls who never gave in to a guy because nobody ever tried anything. But as to sex, what I know about it wouldn't fill a thimble, and what I want to talk about doesn't even exist. So let's skip it.

Dave

Believe it or not, Dad told me dirty jokes. Yeah, it's true. Maybe he figured that way I'd think he was one of the guys. I don't know, maybe he thought that was the way to talk to a kid about it without getting embarrassed. But you'd have to know my dad, I mean, he's Mr. Straight himself, and to have *him* tell *me* dirty jokes (and they weren't funny and I knew better ones) was so crazy I couldn't believe it. And that was all they told me about sex.

They tell you, "Don't pet." They tell you, "Don't neck." But what is petting, what is necking? Touch a girl right here, that's OK. But two inches to the north and you're committing a sin.

They always tell you, don't take advantage of the daughters of Zion. What about the daughters of Zion taking advantage of the *sons* of Zion? I'm not talking about short skirts or anything, either, fella, I'm talking about action, these girls go out on a date, they want action. They know all the ways to turn a guy on — nobody *ever* warns you about that! Took *me* by surprise, that's for sure.

I knew the facts of life, all right. Dad told me. But let's face it — when you're out in that car or by the river on the grass at two in the morning and she wants you and you want her, Dad just isn't standing there to say, "Hold it, stupid, get back in the car." I lost my virginity when I was sixteen. And blessed the sacrament the next day. I didn't even learn how to feel really guilty about it for years afterward. It wasn't until I realized that I wanted to go on a mission that I figured out that I should really feel rotten. I mean, I knew all along that I shouldn't do that, and I really didn't do it except with two girls, but I just kind of shut my mind to that part of the gospel, I kind of said to myself, "Adultery is when you're married. Right now it's only fornication." Ha! I can't believe it, but I actually told myself that.

So that's when my dad became a hero. He and Mom never pushed me about a mission, but they made it clear that the money was there and they hoped I'd go. In those days I was really sharp, Mr. Mormon, because that's pretty much the group I hung around with, and besides, we lived in a Mormon town. The girls I slept with, too, they were Mormon, I wasn't being corrupted by the "world." So I went in to my dad one day and I said, "Dad, I really want to go on a mission."

He looked so proud and happy that I almost didn't go on. But when I set my mind to something, I do it. "Dad," I said, "the trouble is, that I've been sleeping with girls sometimes, and I don't know exactly what I need to do to set it right so I can go." I even had a vague idea that if you had slept with a girl you could never go on a mission.

I've got to hand it to Dad. He didn't get mad or anything. He looked like the world had ended, but he still kept his voice low and quiet and he talked to me really natural then. No dirty jokes this time. But he really said this to me, he said, "I feel like I've failed as a father." What was he supposed to do, come along and hold my hand on *every* date? Let's face it, no matter how much parents love a kid, if he really wants to commit a sin, he's going to commit it. We have our free agency, right? We're individuals, even if we do have parents, so God blames *us* for our sins, not our parents. I knew right from wrong, they had taught me, I just chose wrong!

Anyway, Dad was a real hero then. He just talked to me about it (why hadn't he talked to me before, I wondered?) and then we talked over how much I had done it, and with whom, and whether I was still doing it. He left it up to me what I'd do, but he told me the options, you know, tell the bishop, get the record clear, wait a year, go on a mission. He told me that he'd help me, any way he could. I asked him not to tell Mom, and he said he wouldn't. Since my mission, and after my first marriage ended on the rocks, I told Mom myself, but by then she had figured out that I wasn't exactly the sterling young kid who was always A's in school and was an assistant to the president in the mission field.

That's what kills me. There were kids who weren't given half the opportunity I was who were so much more worthy. I used to doubt the Church because of that: here I am being made secretary of the priests quorum and I'm sleeping with a girl in the next ward twice a week. Where's the inspiration? The bishop is supposed to be inspired. I didn't realize that if you lie to the bishop *he* won't accuse you — but the Spirit will.

Then I finally figured out, the Lord's just giving me enough rope to hang myself. I think I made it sound like it was really easy to repent. It wasn't. It was terrible. Not because it was hard to stop fornicating, because actually that was easy, I just stopped going with those girls. But the closer I got to the Spirit, the more I learned about the gospel, and my Dad was really helping me in that, well, the more I realized how absolutely lousy I had been all those years. I used to read about Alma and going through torment, and even though I'm sure I never felt as bad as he did, I still sometimes thought, "Lord, I'm nothing, I'm awful, please wipe me out completely." He didn't, though. He helped me back up. With my dad's help.

I gotta say, if you don't keep the barn locked and the cows get out, the least you can do is treat 'em nice when they finally come home on their own! That's what my dad did. And it helped a lot.

Cathy

I got all the MIA lessons on chastity. I got the lectures from Mom and Dad about Don't Let Him Try Anything Tell Him You're A Lady If You Let Him Do Anything He Won't Respect You Afterward. So on dates a guy would try something, I'd lift his hand and set it back in his own lap and the date would be over. I was a real jerk about it. Maybe the guy doesn't know any better. Maybe he thinks he's paying you a compliment. I realize now that I could have at least been polite. But I treated a guy who tried anything like the scum of the earth.

I already told you, I married Bill because I had to. This is because of a lot of things, mostly because I really hated the

Church, but that's a whole other thing. Anyway, about the time I was eighteen, I decided the whole thing was a bunch of baloney, I wanted to leave home, forget the parents, forget the Church, cut loose all those chains that were tying me down. I thought that I really hated everything my parents stood for.

And so when I got into drugs and started trying booze and grass and all those things that I'd never tried before, it began to be kind of a game, do all the things your parents hate. So there was this guy in the drug scene, not really in it, I mean Bill was never hooked or anything, but he was with the crowd and smoked grass and drank and everything, but he was a Mormon and still went to church, if you can believe it. Bill was really crazy about me, and on about our third date I just decided that was the night and then we did it. I remember feeling the whole while — I didn't even enjoy it — I was just feeling, "Take that, Mom! Spit in your eye, Dad!" Of course, Bill and I kept doing it, and I got pregnant, and he wasn't the kind of guy — you got to hand it to Bill, even then, he was basically decent, he wasn't going to leave me in the lurch. We talked about it a lot, and after I was about three months along we decided to get married. It broke my parents' hearts when we got married in the court-house. It broke their hearts even more when Emma was born only six months after the wedding. I remember being kind of glad about that at the time. It was so immature of me. Now I know how much a kid can hurt his parents, and the funny thing is, what hurts the parents worst is for the kids to hurt them-selves. I really hurt myself, all the time thinking how smart I was, putting one down on the folks. Talk about stupid!

But that's the thing. My folks always yelled about things. They treated me like I was sleeping around back in the days when I was still turning guys off cold on dates. It doesn't explain anything, but I still think that maybe I wouldn't have gone off the deep end like I did if my parents hadn't always suspected me of doing nasty things and accused me of doing nasty things. I even wrote my mother a letter, sometime before Emma was born but after I was married. It was really short. It said, "Well, Mom, now I'm every lousy thing you always told me I was.

Aren't you proud about being right? Love, Cathy." I thank the Lord I never sent it. I never got to be that cruel.

Todd

One more thing. It isn't hard to be chaste, it really isn't, if you really think about it the right way. This is something my dad said. He said, "It's hard not to fornicate if you're always thinking about how hard you've got to try not to fornicate. But it's easy to stay pure and clean when you always think about how wonderful it's going to be when you go to the temple and hold that woman's hand across the altar and take those vows and start to build a family. Then it would never really cross your mind to put that in jeopardy." I believed that. I still do. It's true.

Listen, Mom and Dad:

1. When you tell us about sex, treat it like something natural. Then it will be easier for us to talk naturally about it to you.

2. Even if the words aren't nice, sometimes you might have to use street language just so we know what you're talking about. At least be *clear*.

3. Don't wait until we're sixteen to talk about sex. It's too late then.

4. After you've taught us right from wrong, if we decide to do something wrong, don't hate yourself. We *are* free agents. If you did your best, it's not your fault.

5. When we do something wrong and come to you for help, don't make us regret talking to you. Be our friends, support us when we need you.

6. Teach us that sex can be beautiful. Teach us how it is supposed to work in a celestial marriage. Don't leave us thinking what the world wants us to think — that it's all dirt.

7. Don't wait for us to ask questions. We might have questions we're scared to ask.

Listen, Mom and Dad . . .

11
about the way
you treated
each other . . .

Children of parents who divorce are more likely to divorce. Children of parents who quarrel are more likely to quarrel. True? Maybe.

But whether they follow the example of your marriage relationship or not, the way you treat each other has a profound effect on them. From their first moment of awareness in the crib until the day they die, the kind of marriage you have, the kind of friendship you have, the way you make decisions, the way you speak to each other, the things you choose to do together and the things you do apart, the way you handle disagreement — you can't hide any of it, not a bit of it, not the tiniest shred, from your children. You can close and lock the door. You can leave the house. You can write each other letters. You can conceal all the details you want.

But your children will know exactly how much you love each other.

Arlene

The way my parents felt about each other! Do you have

time for a horror story? No, it wasn't that bad, I guess. But when I was growing up . . .

One of my earliest memories is of standing with my older brother in the door of our bedroom watching Mom and Dad fight. I don't know what they were fighting about. I couldn't have been more than four or five. I just remember that they kept saying really vicious things to each other. My brother kept saying softly, "That's it, Dad. That's it, Dad." I couldn't tell if he meant, "That's it, you'd better stop," or, "That's it, you tell her." But I know *my* sympathies were all with my mom.

My sympathies were always with my mom until I was old enough to know better.

Don't get me wrong, Mom and Dad didn't *always* fight. They had a lot of good times, and it seemed like they really loved each other a lot of the time. But there were times when I thought they hated each other.

Like that early memory. Mom was screaming and crying about how rotten a husband and father my dad was. Dad was talking really coldly and quietly, furiously, but not raising his voice. He kept saying, "Shut up. Just shut up. I don't want to hear any more."

They both said a swear word. I was really shocked.

And finally Mom slugged Dad right in the stomach. We weren't a very physically demonstrative family — actually hitting somebody was very rare. And when Dad slapped Mom back it was like the end of the world. He slapped her so hard she fell backward, right into the closet, and sat there on a pile of laundry or something. Dad tried to apologize, but she just curled up in the closet and cried and cried. I was crying too, and Dad noticed us watching and told us to go into our rooms and close the door.

There were flare-ups after that, and some of them ended in violence again. For six months we had cardboard over our kitchen window because Mom had thrown a heavy mixing bowl at Dad. Luckily Dad had ducked out of the way and the bowl hit the window instead.

But the big fights, even though they were scary, and even though we kids were really afraid they'd hurt each other badly, the big fights weren't as bad as the little quiet undercover war that went on for the first fifteen years of my life. Longer.

It was Mother's war on men.

When I was little, I remember time after time being told, "Don't you dare go outside alone. Ever ever ever. Some *man* might come along and hurt you." The word *man* was always said as if Mom were saying "viper" or "slime."

If my brother refused to help with the dishes or was even slow about taking out the garbage, my mom would make some little under-her-breath comment about, "That's right, *men* are too good to do the work, it's only *women* who can do the dirty work."

And whenever we kids quarreled or anything else went wrong, somehow — and don't ask me how, I can't remember — but somehow it always got to the point where Mother would find a way to blame it on Dad. It never failed. If I didn't do my homework and got bad grades, it was because my *father* was so busy with his little hobbies and projects that he just didn't have time to help his children, or even to relieve Mother of her load of work so *she* could be a decent mother. If my brother and I fought, somehow it was always because Father hadn't taught us to be polite. If we sassed back to Mom, she'd just storm about how Dad didn't set us the proper example of respect.

I make it sound like my mom was awful. She wasn't. But still, I grew up thinking for years and years that men were somehow bad, were evil, were trying to take advantage of a woman. I remember being so scared of some really nice Mormon guys that even when they tried to be nice to me I shied away.

When I finally realized that Dad wasn't *all* bad and that those things weren't *all* his fault, there was a little while when I really thought I hated my mother. I looked at my life and my phobias and fears and I thought, "Boy, Mom really messed up my life." In a sense, it was true. My parents had such a painful relationship that I had no concept of what a marriage could and should be. And yet, once I realized what was wrong with their marriage, I made the same mistake Mom did: I tried to pin the blame for my problems on someone else instead of trying to solve them.

Finally, after years and years of hating myself and resenting my parents for having such a bad marriage, I realized that I still had only seen part of the picture. There was a lot of stress in those years — financial pressures and debts and my Dad's illnesses. A lot of those problems really *were* my dad's fault: he was a dreamer, he'd always spend today's money because he knew that there'd be a lot of money tomorrow. Only there never was.

And yet in spite of those problems my parents really did love each other. I can see that now that the problems are over.

But even so, I've paid a terrible price for it, I think. And it's hard not to resent them for it.

Dave

My parents always got along great. They never had a quarrel, never had a spat. I can't even remember them seriously disagreeing.

Heaven? Ha.

I'll tell you what I mean — this is a great story. Well, maybe only to me. My mom came home one day and decided she hated the way the living room was. So she took down the curtains, moved the furniture into a big mass in the middle of the room, and called in a few carpet guys to give estimates, looked through a bunch of catalogues, that kind of thing.

I got home from school and I thought a tornado had hit the living room. But Mom was sitting there all involved, with that "serious" look on her face, studying the catalogues.

"Hi, Mom!" I said.

"Don't trip on the lamp cords," she answered.

And then all of a sudden she looked up and said, "Dave, you're home!" I had to agree.

"No, you don't understand, that means your father'll be home in a little while and the house is such a mess!" She looked really concerned about it, as if Dad would make a big fuss about it.

So when Dad came home I made it a point to be right on hand, right there looking on. He walked into the living room, set down his briefcase on the sofa, which was ten feet away from where it usually was, and then walked on out of the room. Not a word. Not a sign that he had even noticed.

At dinner he didn't say anything.

Finally, after he'd spent a few hours in the basement, working on some stuff he had to do for the Sunday School or something, he came upstairs and announced to my mother, "Whatever you're planning, the limit is a thousand dollars and don't use the credit cards, take it out of savings."

And that was the only time he mentioned it.

There were times when I wondered if Dad even noticed Mom was alive for weeks on end. And vice versa. Dad came into the house after work and went straight to some project he had to do. Sometimes Mom was home, sometimes she wasn't, he never asked. And Mom — she was even worse, if possible. She'd never tell anybody when she had a meeting with the Relief Society or some of the city things she was in. I remember she was once in a community theatre play and Dad didn't know about it until he read the review in the paper (which said Mom was awful). He said, "Since when are you in a play?"

"We've been rehearsing since April," Mom said.

"How come you never told me about it?" Dad said, and I've got to admit, he sounded a little perturbed.

"Well, where do you think I've *been* every night for the last two months?"

And the funny thing is, Dad didn't have an answer. I don't think he even noticed she had been *missing* on those nights!

There were times when I wished my parents would just get mad at each other, yell a little, some sign that they even knew each other was alive. Leave each other notes. But never.

Of course, they *slept* together, so I imagine they had good conversations. And whenever there was some really interesting topic of conversation, they got involved in it. But it was as if only the *topic* were interesting — not the person.

Maybe that was part of my problem with Cherie. I was just like my Dad. Even though I was married, I just went right on with my life. I think that next time — if there is a next time, and I hope there is — I'll get a little more involved with the person who decides to share her life with me. Maybe even let her know I care.

LaDell

One of the happiest things about my life — and in case you didn't notice, I'm very, very happy — is that my marriage with Jay is turning out to be every bit as good as my Mom's and Dad's marriage.

I guess I idealized my parents' marriage, but it really does seem ideal to me. They were always deferent to each other. Mom would always ask Dad's opinion before she did anything major — or even minor, sometimes. And Dad would always ask Mom.

I remember that whenever Dad came home, we kids would run to him and he'd give us all a hug. We'd be full of things to say to him, but he'd always say, "In a minute. Where's your mother?"

And we'd say, "In the kitchen." Or wherever.

And then he'd scoop up some of us and the rest would tag along and he'd go wherever Mom was and say, "Arise, O Lady of the Lake, and meet Sir Galahad." Or else, "Ugh. Me want squaw. Where dinner!" Or what were some of the others — just joking things, really affectionate things. And he'd give her a great big kiss, and *then we* could tell Daddy about things.

My most important lesson from my parents' marriage, though, was the way they handled things when they disagreed. They never tried to hide it from us kids. I mean, we got to see the way they arrived at decisions, and they always took our comments seriously, too. For instance, Dad might come home from work and say, "I think it's going to be cheaper to buy a new car than to fix the clunker."

Then Mom would say, "Oh really?"

About fifteen minutes later Mom would say, "Can we afford to buy a new car *and* get the new drapes for the living room?"

Then Dad would say, "That's a thought."

A while later, Dad would say, "I don't think we can afford to do both. But maybe the drapes can wait. Or we could buy the car on time."

Mom would just nod and say, "Those are good points." Then after she had thought awhile, she might say, "Yes, the drapes can wait, and I don't want to get in debt for a car right now." Or she might say, "The drapes are really shabby, honey, and I don't think the car's going to fall apart this week."

Whatever their opinions were, they never contradicted each other right when something was first said. Instead they waited. They thought. They took each other's opinions seriously. They let themselves be influenced by the other person's wishes.

Sometimes they just plain wouldn't reach an agreement. Then Dad would smile and say, "Well, I guess we disagree on that." And Mom would say, "Well, honey, I agree that we certainly do disagree." And then they'd just put off making the decision.

I guess they were lucky or something — they never disagreed seriously on something that had to be decided quickly. But come to think of it, that isn't luck. The really important, urgent decisions they prayed about, and asked for guidance. But the little things, the matters of taste and preference and momentary desires — on those things they either worked out a compromise or put off deciding.

The lesson? Nothing is ever worth getting angry over. No decision is so urgent that it has to be made no matter what damage it does to my marriage.

It never bothered us kids when Mom and Dad disagreed. Because they were always so thoughtful and polite and careful in those discussions, and they treated each other with such respect. And, of course, behind it all we always knew they loved each other.

And Dad brought Mother flowers every now and then for no reason at all. Whenever Mom got flowers like that she'd put them in a vase on the table. And when I came home from school I'd say, "What day is today, Mom?" And she'd say, "Flower day." Flower days were always good days at our house. Of course, I have a hard time remembering days that *weren't* good at our house.

Listen, Mom and Dad:

1. Treat each other kindly and with respect, even when you disagree.

2. There are few things more frightening to us than what seems to be hatred between the two most important people in our world.

3. Never, never use us as pawns in your quarrels with each other.

Listen, Mom and Dad . . .

12
the only reason I didn't get where you wanted me to go was because I'm going somewhere else

Your goals for your children are not necessarily their goals for themselves. Your job is not to teach them every step they should take in life. Your job is to teach them to be kind and loving and righteous along the way, to help them choose paths that will lead them back to God. But it's your children who must choose a career, an educational level, a spouse, their real interests and hobbies. You shouldn't try to force your own will on them in these matters — and very few parents *deliberately* do.

But accidentally, parents can exert tremendous pressure sometimes.

You can't make an athlete out of an academic unless he wants to. You can't make a socialite out of a solitary person unless he wants to. You can't force a happy marriage on your children. . . . You can't make a child care about English literature when all he wants is music.

The old saying is, you can't make a silk purse out of a sow's ear. But when you try to make your children fulfil your goals instead of their own, you're trying to make a sow's ear out of a silk purse. Even if you could do it, you wouldn't like what you'd get when you were through.

Reuben

Dad wanted to be a doctor, but because he had a bad eye he couldn't get into medical school. Instead he did shift work at a steel plant. Eventually he got pretty high up and had a desk and everything, but for years and years he did heavy manual labor. He came home from work dripping wet with sweat and heat from the mills, his hands filthy, his clothes a mess, his hair all tousled from being under a hard hat all day.

Every now and then, even when I was little, he'd say to me, "Don't be dumb like your father. Go to school. Get the grades."

OK, that's fine, that's what everybody says. But some of us just don't have all that much in the way of brains. No, not that I'm dumb, but I just don't *care* that much. At least, I didn't then. I wanted to have fun a little, too.

I remember in high school I wanted to get a job. A friend of mine was a cook at a smorgasbord place at night. There was an opening. I was old enough, and I just mentioned that I thought I'd get this job.

You would've thought I'd said I was going to apostatize from the Church or something. Dad just hit the roof. He went into the bedroom and pulled out all my old report cards and spread them out on the table and said, "C, B, D, B-, C, B," which was pretty much how my grades went in high school. "With grades like that, Rube, you want to get a job? When do you plan to study?"

And then he'd go into this long speech. You want me to recite it word for word? I can do it. It never changed. It goes like this:

"All my life I've had to make my living with my hands and my arms and my back, sweating like an animal, like a pack horse, coming home like a beast in the field after plowing all day. Nobody ever said to me, 'What do you think?' Always I've been treated like an idiot. You want to know why? No diploma. No college, nothing. Well, that's not going to happen to any kid of mine. You're going to college. You're going to make money.

You're going to work behind a desk. You're going to come home smelling like you just got through with your shower. You're going to have people call you 'Sir' and ask your opinion and jump when you say 'Jump.' I didn't work my tail off for twenty years to have my kids end up a jerk like me."

That's the speech. Only it went on for about two hours, the same thing over and over.

Once my older brother Tom said to him, "Dad, I like you. I *want* to grow up to be a jerk just like you."

But everybody knew it was a joke. You want to know the roster, the whole list? Everybody in my family has gone to college. Everybody in my family has got at least one degree, except me — even my little sister. Everybody who's working is making over twenty thou a year, and those who aren't working are having a lot of babies and their *husbands* are making over twenty thou a year.

But the truth is, see, I really didn't *care* about school. I liked working with my hands. I liked doing physical type jobs, you know, tinkering around with my Yamaha, cooking at the restaurant, driving a truck, I've done a lot of different jobs.

Dad's just never been able to understand it. Before my mission he made me feel like I was sinning because I earned my own money. Whenever I came home with a new sweater or something that I'd bought with my own money, he'd say something like, "That's a nice sweater," and then he'd say to my Mom, loud so I'd be sure to hear it, "If he wanted a sweater, he could have asked me."

Why should I ask him? I had the money. I wasn't working because I didn't have enough money from Dad. I was working because I liked to work. I liked the guys and girls I worked with, you know? It was fun. School was a drag.

I moved out of my parents' house the year before my mission because I was so fed up with the constant questions and pressure. "How're you doing in your psych class, your English class, your engineering class," on and on far into the night. "Are you going to get another D? How come you don't study anymore, last time you got Ds."

And so I started lying to them. I mean, if I said, "I'm doing really lousy in my psych class because I don't go to it very much," I'd get a two-hour lecture on why college was important. If I said, "I don't care if I get a D," Dad would give me a two-hour lecture on why college means money and part of growing up is learning how to do things even when you don't enjoy them.

So it was easier to just say, "Hey, everything's going great." After my freshman year they didn't send my grades to my folks. When I went on my mission, I had been kicked out of my college for low grades. My folks didn't even know. My last semester before my mission I just worked, saved money. It really hurt my Dad's feelings that I never asked him for a cent to support me on my mission. Other parents are proud when their sons pay for their own mission. But Dad just thought I was thumbing my nose at him or something.

On my mission I did some growing up, like everybody else. I decided school mattered, I didn't want to drift around. But when I came back, what college would take me? I know, it's my own fault, and I've paid for it by having to take a whole bunch of correspondence courses to make up for the classes I flunked out of. But I can't help thinking that if Dad had just let me work instead of pushing and pushing for me to go to college, I would have liked him better before I left — and now, when I'm ready to start school, I wouldn't have to make up for a grade point average that's hanging down around zero.

I mean, so what if Dad worked all his life? Maybe I *like* to work. It's no skin off his nose, is it? But he always had to push us to go to school whether we liked it or not. Oh well.

And now when he sees how hard I'm working, he keeps saying, "See? Why didn't you study like that three years ago!" But I don't get mad. I just study.

LaDell

It was really funny. When I got to college and really worked at it, I think my parents were disappointed. All during high school they had been so proud of my nearly straight A's and the artwork and the drama and the flute solos with the orchestra and everything. They thought it was so wonderful.

Then I got to college and my mother would look at those report cards with straight A's on them and *sigh.* I'd spend a whole night slaving over a clay rough of a sculpture and Mother would say, "Some people go on dates, some people make mud pies."

Dad would tell unmarried young guys in the ward to ask me out. Really! Oh, no, he wouldn't twist their arms, I was pretty popular. But I kept turning down dates because I was *busy.* And then Mom and Dad would look at each other in despair. It was really funny.

Except that they were very serious. I was only nineteen years old when they decided I was going to be an old maid. I wasn't meeting enough boys. I wasn't dating enough boys.

"Mom," I'd say. "Dad, I don't *want* to meet boys. I don't *want* to date boys. I want to meet *men.* I want to date *men.*"

They'd make comments about how I was so picky I'd never find a man good enough for me and I'd end up regretting it.

And all the time, all I really cared about was sculpting. I know — the Church teaches you're supposed to get married. I never planned on *not* getting married. It's just that I had discovered that I had talent. I could really do a good job. But not good enough: I had so much to learn. And it meant a lot to me to learn it.

So I did — because I'm basically a mule, you know. When I want to do something, I *do* it.

So I kept right on, got my bachelor of fine arts degree and then got about ten offers from design firms — even though I was a sculptor, my work for my design and two-dimensional art classes was good enough that they wanted me.

But here's the funniest part. I turned them all down flat. Because I wasn't after a great career — especially not in design. I was after learning how to sculpt. And even though I'll never be a Michelangelo, I'm pretty good and getting better all the time.

It was right after I had turned down all those jobs that I met Jay. We were married three months after we met. A time for everything, and everything in its time, that's what I say.

But Mom and Dad never really caught on. They were so *relieved.* Even at my wedding, my Mom put her arm around me and said, "Now, LaDell, isn't this so much *better?*"

Than what? My life has gone the way I wanted it to go all along. They just never believed that I knew where I was going, I guess.

Cathy

Goals! My parents decided that I only had one goal in life — to go directly to the devil, do not pass go, do not collect two hundred dollars. They used to get so uptight about the stupidest things. I mean, OK, rock music wasn't what they grew up with. That didn't mean they had to ridicule it constantly. It was bad enough that I had to keep my radio so soft I couldn't hear it or somebody would yell, "Turn down that noise." But then at dinner, time after time, Mom or Dad would say — out of the clear blue — "I can't get over the trash you teenagers listen to. 'Oh Bebe, Ah love-a you, oh Bebe, oh Bebe.' " It made me sick. It was just so obvious that they never even *listened* to it. They kept talking about how it was all filthy and vile and silly — but how can anyone call Simon and Garfunkel silly? Or Joni Mitchell? I mean, sure, there are really junky groups, but I had taste. There was good rock music and bad rock music, just like there's good classical music and bad classical music. It's just that nobody plays the bad classical stuff much anymore. Though if you ask me, Mozart is a drag.

And if you listen to the words to the songs from my parents' generation it'll make you laugh. I mean, they sing about "Baby" and "I love you" and all those silly ways of saying things every bit as much as AM-radio rock music does. So what? Who cares? I never mocked them and their tastes. Why did they mock mine? It didn't make me change my tastes at all. It just convinced me that they not only didn't know what they were talking about, but also that they had no respect for my opinions and desires.

Same thing with clothing styles. OK, I was in my teens during the miniskirt period. What did they want me to do, go to school looking like an idiot? The only girls who ever wore knee-length dresses — and I'm talking about good Mormons, too — were the jerky-looking ones who also never washed their hair. I never wore an *extreme* miniskirt — at least, not at first. But if the dress was over my knee it was World War II all over again. I was showing off my body to evil-minded men. I was breaking the commandments. I was sinful. I was rebellious.

Didn't they look at the other girls? Didn't they realize that I had a choice between being a weirdo and getting along with my parents or being normal and having my parents yell at me all the time? It was so dumb. They never looked at it as a matter of *degree.* My skirts were short, yes. But how short? Not very. And compared to the other girls, I was pretty doggone conservative — at first.

But after a while I got so sick of the stupid battles over things that were so silly, I just started raising all my hems just to get them mad. It was childish of me, but my attitude was, "If they thought *that* was immodest, wait till they see *this.*"

It never occurred to them that maybe the only reason I didn't dress the way they thought I should was because I was living in a different world. We're supposed to be in the world, but not of it. Fine. But all they accomplished by trying to make me conform to the standards of 1948 was to make me rebel for real.

I know, nobody can *make* you rebel. I did that on my own. But if they hadn't tried to push me, if they hadn't tried to lock me in that tight little prison of *their* tastes and *their* judgments, I wouldn't ever have gone as far as I did the other way.

And yet, in a sense, they succeeded. They wanted my life to be completely centered around their standards. Well, it worked. Only instead of being centered around *obeying* those standards, I was centered around *disobeying* them.

That's the ridiculous thing. My parents acted as if they could actually make me do what they wanted. When I was little, they could. But by the time a kid is sixteen or seventeen, she can do whatever she wants. She may have to hide it, but her parents just aren't going to be able to stop her. The only way they could have influenced me at that time was by loving me and being a friend — heaven knows I needed real friends. But instead they just closed every door because I refused to do exactly what they wanted on what were, really, very minor things. And because I was the rebellious, stubborn child that I was, the very things they most feared came true. Completely unnecessarily.

Listen, Mom and Dad:

1. Don't decide for us what we should want. We'll decide for ourselves anyway, and all you'll accomplish by pushing is to drive us away.

2. If there's something you think is important for us, try to make it look attractive.

3. Don't make yourself into an enemy. Don't mock our desires. Respect them.

4. Look closely. Maybe what we're doing isn't really bad — maybe it's just different.

13
I was
wrong and
I'm sorry

There are so many things we kids did that hurt you. We may not have known it at the time, but we know it now. Will it help if we tell you that we're sorry? Will it help if we tell you that we learned from it? Will you forgive us if you know that we love you even more now because of how close we thought we came to losing your love?

LaDell

It'll probably seem like such a little thing, but I'm sure it hurt my parents a great deal. My folks weren't rich by any means. There were financial problems. And one Christmas — I think I was about nine — things were really tight. But that year they were coming out with the first talking *and* walking dolls. The ones that you just let go and they walked all around the room, you know? To me that was magic, the end of the world, and on my letter to Santa Claus I only put one thing: a walking doll. And I made it a point to tell my parents, too, as often as possible.

Well, on Christmas morning there was a doll. Only instead of being the kind that walked all by itself, it only walked if you held its hand and kind of pulled it along. Dad showed me how it worked, and they tried to get me excited about it, but I just acted like a little pig. I pouted and wouldn't play with it. I didn't play with anything all Christmas day. It was the silliest thing, and I knew even while I was doing it that it was completely selfish.

But my parents didn't get angry or anything. They kept inviting me to take part in all the family activities, and finally (ah, the great self-sacrifice!) I went in and like a martyr took part in the games, pausing every now and then to sigh in self-pity.

And the next year — this is what I find hard to believe about myself — in my letter to Santa Claus I wrote, "And this year I want a doll that walks *all by itself*."

My parents were wise enough not to give it to me. It wasn't until I thought back on that, years later, that I realized that that Christmas my parents must have felt terrible, because I'm sure they had wracked their brains trying to think of how they could afford to give me such an expensive present — and even the doll whose hand you had to hold wasn't cheap. And yet their child proved so ungrateful — well, I just wish I hadn't done that. I hope they know that *now* I understand, and I'm grateful for everything they did for me, because I know they always did their best.

Todd

What do I wish I could do over again? I'd take advantage of the piano lessons and the tennis lessons and the dancing lessons and the swimming lessons and all the opportunities my parents gave me. Back then I always looked at each of those projects as something I had to put up with because I was still small and had to do what my parents said. They always told me, "Todd, just try it for three months. If you work really hard, you'll enjoy it, we promise."

But I never worked really hard. So here I am, a twenty-six-year-old nonpianist who can't play tennis, can't dance, and swims like a crippled rhinoceros.

But there it is — you can lead a kid to lessons but you can't make him care!

Dave

For about six months or a year or something after my mission, my Mom would every now and then drop a little hint: "Dave, the Lord will really bless you if you pay a full tithing." "Dave, you're so bright, you could really be an asset to a priesthood quorum, if you'd only get up on Sunday mornings." "Dave, the Lord has given you so much. Where much is given much is expected."

I knew what she was getting at. She thought I was drifting away from the Church. Well, that was ridiculous. I was keeping track of my tithing, I'd make it up when I missed a month or two. I had a testimony — could I help it if I worked late on Saturday nights? And it's not as if the bishop were beating down my door to get me to participate in Church or anything. I was active! I was a believing, practicing Latter-day Saint.

It wasn't until Cherie filed for divorce that I actually stood back and looked at my life and realized that I hadn't been to Church more than twice during the year of my marriage, that I hadn't paid any tithing at all for over a year, that I was thinking — and talking — negatively about the Church and about Church leaders, that I was, to put it briefly, a totally inactive Mormon.

I remember the day Cherie's lawyer brought the papers to my office. After he left I just stared at the walls. One of the things I remembered really clearly was my Dad saying, "Going inactive is so easy, Dave. All you have to do is nothing. And pretty soon you turn into nothing." Well, that's what I was. Nothing.

And yet the day my Dad said that, I had flown into a rage, I had slammed the door and left the house and squealed the tires of my MG and driven up into the hills and not come back until late at night. I remember yelling as I left the house, "It doesn't matter whether you think I have a testimony or not, the Lord knows I have one and he's the only one that matters."

I wish I could tell my parents — but I think they know. They were right. And I knew all along they were right. I was just trying to fool myself and them into thinking that the way I was going was right. It wasn't right. It was just easy.

I wish I'd listened back then, though.

Cathy

I've done about everything wrong that a kid could do wrong. And I've paid for it, believe me.

All the time I was doing it I really thought I hated my parents. And it's partly true, anyway: they really did make some big mistakes in dealing with me. But I know that now they blame themselves for my failures and my mistakes. I can hear my mother saying, "Where did I fail her?"

Well, they didn't fail me. I failed myself. Sure, they meddled and they pushed and they pried and they made me mad. But it wasn't their fault when I started sleeping with men. It wasn't their fault when I chose to do everything that I had ever been taught was wrong. I knew I was sinning and I knew it was serious.

They said and did a lot of things that hurt me. Well, I got even. I hurt them far worse than they ever did me. And in the process I hurt myself. I just wish there were some way to go back in the past and erase all that, just tear it up and start over. I wish it were enough just to say, "Mom and Dad, I'm sorry, you were right."

But I think the reason I don't say that is because I'm afraid they'd answer, "Of course we were right, Cathy. We told you so."

I wish I were sure they would put their arms around me and say, "Cathy, we're so glad you realize your mistakes, because we also realize our mistakes. We shouldn't have gotten so angry at you over little things. We shouldn't have yelled at you all the time, and we're sorry for our mistakes, too."

That's still my selfish streak. I can't yet be big enough to ask for forgiveness without having an apology offered in return.

But for what it's worth, I really *am* sorry that I hurt them so badly. I wish I hadn't. I hope they know that, and that I still love them in spite of all the poison we've had between us over the years.

Listen, Mom and Dad:

1. Chances are pretty good that somewhere along the line we'll look back and say, "You know, Mom and Dad were right."

2. Just don't ever say to us, "Someday down the line, you're going to look back and regret that you didn't listen to us." When it happens, then we'll know. Till it does, we won't believe it. After all, we're just kids.

Listen, Mom and Dad . . .

14
thanks
for the
memories

Admit it. Hanging up the stockings was as much fun for you as it was for us. Ah, but it *was* fun for us. And the trips we took together, and the big hoopla about birthdays, and the little things that came from time to time, the traditions.

Singing in the car on the way to church.

Playing Pull-Down-Daddy.

Drawing family murals, everybody covered with crayon and smiles.

Those traditions were a gift of love that we can hardly wait to pass on to our own families.

Arlene

Mother has always loved to sing. She never really had any formal training, but she told us kids how she loved music when she was growing up. I can't remember a time when Mother didn't have a song for us.

Often it was the old songs. I remember that every trip we took was full of songs. From the years when Mom was a little girl,

like "In a Little Spanish Town," and "It Happened in Monter-
rey," and fun ones like the song about the fish — "Dit Dit
Dattum Dattum Wattum, Choo" — how in the world do you
spell that? I can still sing them all, every word.

It would be night, and Dad would be driving along, and to
keep Dad awake — and because we kids always asked for the
songs — Mother would start singing a song. We'd join in
whenever we knew the words. "If I were the only girl in the
world and you were the only boy," that was a favorite; I think it
was the first song I ever learned. She'd sing softly, even though
in church she sometimes sang solos that made the whole room
ring with sound, but in the car she sang soft and sweet and we
could hear our own voices.

And harmony. Once we knew the songs, she'd harmonize,
and oh, that was magic. We learned how to do that, too — I
remember my older brother and I singing two different parts of
harmony along with Mom on the melody. We just made it up as
we went along.

Mom turned it into a game to keep us busy. We once had an
improvised contest — Mom offered to pay us a penny a hymn
for as many as we could sing all the way through (one verse, that
is). I think I got a quarter.

But the part about Mother's singing that I like best of all —
and the younger kids don't remember this, because for some
reason Mom stopped — was the way she made up songs for my
older brother and me. I was very, very little. She would sing
things like, "Arlene has been such a good girl today, she helped
Mommy do the dishes, and she picked up her own toys, and
even though she had a quarrel with her brother she said I'm
sorry and gave him a hug. I love Arlene a whole, whole lot."
The words were never the same, but they always were about
me, and always were about my day. I would make up songs and
sing back to her. Mom stopped doing that when I was five. I
don't know why. Maybe I or my brother said something about
how we were too old for that kind of thing. Maybe we started

thinking it was silly. But looking back, I loved that. If I ever marry and have children, I'm going to sing to them that way.

Because singing is to talking the way a caress is to a gesture. Sure, all the time you talk you make gestures, you wave your hands around, but it's just ordinary, you know? But then every now and then you reach out a hand and touch someone, really gently, in a way that says "I love you."

Singing was Mother's way of caressing me with her voice.

Reuben

What I remember best about my Dad was the playing around. Rough-and-tumble stuff, you know. Like picking us up by one arm and one foot and swinging us around like an airplane, making us go high and then go low. We'd get so dizzy! But it was a great ride, better than anything they ever had at a carnival. He was so big he could have one of us piggy-back, and still pick up three more, two under one arm and one under the other, and truck us around the house like that, or out in the yard.

And wrestling. Dad was strong, but still he let us win enough — never win the whole wrestling game, of course, but he'd let us pull him down, and then pummel him a little, so we felt like it was fair. He'd just laugh, though, when he was through playing, and pin us so fast. But the game couldn't end unless we said "uncle." If he was tired and we weren't, we'd just refuse to say "uncle" and he'd have to stay there. Sometimes he'd make a "mistake" and let us get away and the match would go on. But if he really was through, he'd tickle us until we said "uncle." Tickling could get us to say "uncle" faster than anything.

Dad wasn't all that hot at regular sports, but he could hit a ball all right and throw and catch in the front yard. I know, everybody supposedly has a father who teaches them to play ball, but you'd be surprised how few fathers actually do. Dad would get out the ball and we'd run out into the front yard — and he always ran out yelling, you know, like Tarzan, and so

would we — out would come all of us yelling like we were
savages about to scalp the entire neighborhood.

Then all of us would cut out to different places — across the
street, the other corner of the yard — and Dad would throw.
Usually we'd throw back to Dad, but sometimes we'd surprise
each other by throwing to someone else. If we dropped the ball
everybody would yell in unison, "Butterfingers." It wasn't
mean, it was just a joke. Even now, whenever somebody in the
family drops something at a family get-together, we all yell,
"Butterfingers," and everybody laughs.

But we never — I mean, nobody ever yelled "butterfingers"
at a little kid in the family. The little kid was usually me — I've
only got one younger than me, and she's a girl, so nobody
expected her to catch very good. But nobody ever yelled "butterfingers" at me. They'd just yell "great catch" when I caught
something.

Maybe it was because I was a boy, but Dad meant a lot to
me. He wasn't home all that often — he did shift work a lot, you
know, for weeks on end we wouldn't see him between getting
home from school and going to bed at night. But when he was
home, man, he was important.

My memory of Mom is really dim, you know? Not dim, like
faded out, but dim like those shots in the movies. I just kind of
see her as if the sun was shining through the curtains and she
was standing there in the kitchen with the sun behind her. She
was always so busy. But she was always there, you know? In the
background, maybe, unnoticed sometimes, but *there*.

When I cried, Dad would just kind of stand there, helpless,
because he didn't know how to handle it except by maybe
teasing me out of it. But Mom knew just how to put her arms
around a guy so he didn't feel like he was a Momma's boy, but
he still felt *better*. And she didn't say anything at those times.
Just held on tight. That's what I remember best about my Mom
and Dad.

Todd

Family days. Christmas most of all, but other family days, too. Every birthday was a party, was special. And they were always family days. If we had a birthday party that our friends came to, that was separate from the family party.

On birthdays, the birthday boy or the birthday girl — I guess that sounds silly, now, but it was sure special then — the kid having the birthday didn't have to do any work at all. Sometimes we'd even get breakfast in bed, served up by the whole family tootling on imaginary horns and stuff. That wasn't often, but sometimes. The real party was at the birthday dinner. Then there'd be Dad with the old camera taking pictures, and a cake. The birthday kid got to choose the menu for the dinner — I remember once asking for ravioli, tamales, spaghetti, and tacos all in the same meal. Also he got to choose what flavor cake. I always chose spice cake with caramel icing.

All through dinner there'd be this stack of presents by the birthday person, and everybody would keep saying, "Isn't it about time you opened another present?" The birthday person had a hard time getting any dinner! But each present got a special opening, and because everybody was eager to see what was in the packages the birthday person always had a lot of attention. It's a family joke now. I mean, right after the blessing on the food it's "for pete's sake, stop eating and open a present already."

And when we were little the whole evening was spent playing games. The birthday boy or birthday girl got to choose the games. If it was a little kid, that meant playing blockhead and hot-and-cold and Matthew-Mark-Luke-John and all the other old games. If it was an older kid, it meant charades or twenty questions or table games, things like that.

In fact, that was the hardest time on my mission. My birthdays; you know? Silly. But when it was my birthday, I just kind of looked around and didn't see any family. It wasn't the presents I missed, it was the people, it was the fuss about you, it was the way you knew that you were loved and important. I know it sounds silly, but even my second birthday in the mission field, when I was a zone leader and thought I was very, very mature, I cried myself to sleep on the night of my birthday.

No, not because it was so awful there in the mission field. It was because I really missed my family. And on my birthday I remembered it most of all because it was always such a day of love.

And another thing. My parents were really serious about it being a family day. We rarely had anybody besides family over. I remember when I was twelve wanting to invite a pretty good friend over. My mom asked me really seriously, "Is he such a good friend that he should be part of a family day?" I thought about it for a while, and then I decided that he really wouldn't fit in to the kind of day we have as a family. But later on, when I was sixteen, I had a really close friend who *did* fit in with the family, who fit right in, like a brother, and who I loved like a fourth brother. And my parents were glad to have him come.

And my wife, Rachel. It was practically my declaration of serious intentions toward her when I invited her to come to a family day.

My parents told me later that that was when they knew Rachel and I would get married — because that was when they realized I loved her enough and felt comfortable enough with her to consider her part of the family. And so I remember my mom and dad opened up their arms and hugged her, right there in the living room. And when I realized that I wasn't embarrassed to have that happen, I knew that I'd chosen right. I mean, I was always so *comfortable* with my family — if somebody fit in with them, why, they couldn't help but fit in with me, right?

Cathy

My favorite memory is the night that we climbed the roof. We were living in Arizona then. We had air conditioning like everyone else, but one night it went on the blink, just pooped out, and it was so *hot*. At first we left all the windows closed to try to keep in the cool air, but pretty soon it was too hot, and then we opened the windows to try to catch any breezes, but there wasn't a breeze anywhere.

We were all tossing and turning and getting sweaty and sticky hot, and nobody could sleep.

So at ten-thirty Dad got out of bed and roared at the top of his voice, "It's too hot in this horrible house!"

"Shhh!" Mom said. "You'll wake up the kids."

"They're all awake anyway," Dad said back. "Aren't you, kids!"

And we all were. So Dad went roaring through the house at the top of his voice. "Get the sleeping bags, get the tarpaulin, we're going on an expedition, we're not going to sleep in this horrible hot house!"

So we all gathered everything up. It was so exciting, holding onto a pillow and a sheet and going outside in pajamas and bedroom slippers. Dad and my older brother, Rod, went up on the roof on the ladder and spread out the sleeping bags, all opened up to make one huge bed. We were on the side of the roof where we were hidden from the street.

Then Dad left Rod on the roof and came down for us. He got me near the top of the ladder and then Teddy in the middle and Jimmy at the bottom, and then he'd call out, "Sheets up!" and point to one of us, and that person would hand his sheet up the ladder until Rod got it at the roof and put it on one of the sleeping bags. After the sheets it was "pillows up!" and then finally he said, "Up with all the little people!"

"Up with little Cathy!" which made us laugh because I was probably eleven and I was taller than Rod already. Then "up with little Teddy" and "up with little Jimmy." It was kind of scary on the roof. The ground looked really far, but the roof wasn't steep at all, so there was no danger of falling off, even if we rolled in our sleep, and there was this kind of wall thing along the edge of the roof, anyway.

Then Dad called out, "Up with little Mommy!" which we all laughed at including Mom because she was already a little overweight then. But she's a good sport, I've got to hand that to her, and she was right up the ladder with us.

Dad came up last of all, and then he asked us, "Well, do we leave the ladder down, or do we pull it up in case the Indians attack in the night?"

We all voted for the ladder to be up, because it was fun to pretend we were in a fort.

We all slept with sheets over us. We got horrible mosquito bites. The sleeping bags got roof gravel in them. We all woke up early with stiff backs. It was so wonderful that for years afterward we'd every now and then say, "Let's sleep on the roof. Who wants to sleep in this horrible hot house?" But we never did. Probably because Mom and Dad knew that the second time would never be quite the same.

Dave

My favorite memory of my parents?

How do you pick? This day was my favorite — that's impossible. I've been kind of a creep a lot of my life, but there are a lot of good days to remember, too. I can't pick one day!

No, I *can* pick one day. It was the day after my cousin Jack died. He was fourteen years old and a wonderful guy. I remember looking up to him and wishing my older brother was like him. He was the only person I ever let tickle me. And my mom and dad used to tell us how he was such an obedient boy, not to compare us to him, because they never said it when we had been misbehaving. No, I think it was just because Jack was really somebody special — I hate that word, *special,* but this time it's the only word that says it. He stood out. He was unique.

Uncle Don and Aunt Mary lived on a farm back then, an orchard. Their kids started driving the tractor at about age twelve. Anyway, Jack was driving the tractor through the orchard one day, doing some job or other, and in backing up the tractor he forgot to change gears or forgot to look behind him or something. But he hit his head on a tree branch and was knocked out and the tractor kept backing up and he was crushed to death against the tree. Uncle Don found him.

We got the phone call in the middle of the night, and that very night Mom and Dad got us all out of bed and told us the news. Mom and Dad were crying, both of them, and we knew it was serious. But we really didn't understand death, at least I didn't. Maybe my older sister Annie did, because she was really somber, but Val and I didn't get what was going on. Dying was something army men in the movies did.

We got in the car and started driving. We drove all night and got to Don's and Mary's farm at about 5:00 A.M. Because it was still so early, Mom and Dad discussed whether to wait for a while or go right to their house. We waited for an hour. Then, with most of us kids still sleepy, we drove up their driveway, a long dirt road with an orchard on both sides, and came to their white frame house. There were already lights on, so we weren't waking them up.

At first for me it was a lark. I got to sleep in my cousin Harry's bed with him — he's my age — and we talked and played around the farm all morning and afternoon and caught frogs. I was a city boy, and this was the first time I had spent any time on a farm at all.

All that day there was the sound of laughter of little children all around the house. We kids entertained each other.

Mealtimes we came inside. My mother fixed the meals, mostly, but Aunt Mary insisted on helping. After all, she knew where everything was. My mother didn't argue, just kept talking on and on about cheerful things, about talks she had heard recently in church, about politics, about the crops there on the farm, about anything that popped into her head. And Aunt Mary joined in sometimes, and smiled sometimes. At the time I didn't understand, but I do now. My mother was giving Aunt

Mary stability. She was being confident and sure, and because she was there Aunt Mary didn't fall apart.

I found out later that all that day Uncle Don and Dad were together making the funeral arrangements, getting the coffin bought and the gravesite purchased and making sure the body was ready for the burial.

Why is this my favorite memory? I don't know — but it really stuck with me. It was that night. We kids were getting tucked into bed in the basement. Aunt Mary was tucking in Harry, and Mom was tucking me in. And they both kissed us goodnight, but it was long and hard.

Then as they were leaving the little partitioned area where we were sleeping, Mom suddenly stopped and put her arms around Aunt Mary and just started to cry. She said, over and over, "Mary, I loved Jack so much. I loved him so much."

It's funny, but that seemed to be the perfect thing, the right and kind and good thing to say. Because even though she was crying, too, Aunt Mary was able to hold my mother and kind of rock her back and forth and say, "Did you really? He was a good boy, wasn't he?"

Harry and I just lay there watching them. They held onto each other so tightly.

Whenever I think of real true undying love, I remember that night in the basement of my Uncle Don's farmhouse. Because instead of always holding back and staying "in control," Mom was able to let go of herself and hold onto someone else, and let that someone else hold onto her, too. Mom was saying, in her own way, "You aren't the only one who has lost Jack. We have all lost him. But at least we *had* him."

That night I got up in the middle of the night to go to the bathroom. I went upstairs. And then, because the night was dark and I was afraid, I went into the living room, where Mom and Dad were sleeping on the fold-out couch. I went up and touched Mom, and she made a sleepy noise. I think I was only six at the time, maybe younger.

I said, "Mom, if I died would you cry like you cried for Jack tonight?"

She put her arm around me and held me tight against the side of the bed and said, "I'd cry even more, Dave, because you're my own little boy."

That day is my favorite memory because I learned how deep love goes.

LaDell

Christmas. The whole rigmarole. Hanging the stockings, decorating the tree — we kids were always part of it from beginning to end. Christmas began in our family even before the stores started advertising. We'd ask Mom what she was making — clear back in August. And she'd say, "An apron for Grandma Parker," or "hot pan holders for the ward bazaar."

Christmas was always a big thing, but Santa Claus was only part of it. My parents tell me that when I was a baby, only two or three, they had a tree and presents under it, a whole lot of them, and because my little brother was only one, most of them were for me. But they had them all be from Santa Claus, and only one present from them. They tell me that all of a sudden, as I was playing with my new toys, I looked up and said, "Mommy and Daddy, didn't *you* give me anything?"

So from then on, Santa Claus only brought one gift for each child, plus whatever was in the stocking. And the gift Santa brought wasn't even the biggest gift — the biggest always came from Mom and Dad.

And we kids always gave presents to each other. There are five of us. As soon as we started catching the Christmas spirit from Mom and Dad, we'd save all our allowance, and buy as many gifts for each other as we could. Especially the older kids, the ones who "knew." For us, the excitement of Christmas was giving to each other. I guess we spent every penny for almost half the year on buying gifts for other people. I can't think of a better use for the money.

We all had our secret places for hiding our presents. And Mom and Dad made it a really important rule for no one to try to peek. "What good is it for someone to try to surprise you if you're going to ruin their surprise?" It was almost as if our surprise and fun at getting a gift were the best way of saying thank you.

Because of the huge number of presents, the pile spread from one wall to the other. Daddy took forever passing out the presents one by one. We'd all sit there on Christmas morning and watch while the presents were opened. We took turns, all the while wondering what was in *that* box or *this* box, and laughing delightedly when one of our brothers and sisters or when Mom or Dad were really excited and happy about their gifts.

I remember the gifts I gave even better than the gifts I got.

The best part of Christmas, though, was when I was twelve and I finally asked Mom and Dad, "If there isn't a Santa Claus, then *who* fills the stockings?" They told me, and then I said, "Who fills *your* stockings?"

"We do," they said.

"Not this year," I told them.

So after they had gone to bed I got up and sneaked into the living room and found their stockings there. They had taken me very seriously — nothing was in their stockings except the fruits and nuts and candy — the little presents weren't there at all.

I had spent my whole supply of last-minute Christmas money on those little gifts. I suppose some of them were pretty silly. But I was so proud to be Santa Claus to my Mom and Dad. And they had trusted me to do it right.

After that, it was sort of our initiation into adulthood to be able to help with the secret things of Christmas. And finally, when all of us were in our teens or older, Mom and Dad went to bed *before* the oldest kids, and we did the big surprises. Like when three of us chipped in together to give Dad thirty dollars to buy a pair of shoes. We got it in one-dollar bills and paper-clipped them to a string that we hung between the tree and a lamp. Or the time we bought Mom a new heavy winter coat and made a ridiculous dummy out of newspapers so that when she came in on Christmas morning, there was this dummy sitting on the couch with crossed legs — wearing her coat and her extra pair of glasses.

They always made us kids wait in the kitchen until we could all march into the living room where the tree was, youngest first. Dad took movies. Sometimes (oh, the frustration of seeing the tree and the beautiful lights and presents and having to *leave* again!) he'd made us go back out and come in again because he got the exposure wrong!

And on Christmas we always played with each other. Somehow we got the hint from Mom and Dad that toys were no fun unless somebody helped you play with them. So we'd take turns trying out the new toys, playing with brothers and sisters all day. And all the next day.

There was rarely a Christmas let-down feeling because even though we built up to Christmas for months and months, the climax was not in *getting,* but in *giving.* And so we continued to have Christmas whenever we saw someone using the gift we had given them.

The best part of Christmas, though, was the Christmas play. We always acted out the story of the birth of Jesus. I was usually Mary, though once I was the innkeeper and several times I was the angel. There was always prompting from Mom and Dad, of course. But we'd get all decked out in bathrobes and do the whole story from beginning to end. When we were little it was a lot of fun. When we were older it started getting very sacred.

Now that there aren't any little ones, we just read the story to each other. But we still take parts. And now I have such a strong testimony of the Savior, and that combined with my great love for my family and the beauty of that peaceful evening before

Christmas day always makes me cry. It's silly — I'm crying now just thinking about it. Oh, well. You asked for my favorite memory, and that was just begging for tears.

I love the Savior. I love my family. And I'm so grateful to my parents for teaching me both those loves.

Listen, Mom and Dad:

1. We remember love.

2. Traditions stick with us and are treasured, even though we don't particularly tell you.

3. If you ever have the impulse to do something with the family, something fun or different or exciting, do it. It lasts forever.

15
when I was afraid
you held
my hand

We came as strangers into the world. It was scary. Sometimes even now we get frightened — perhaps you still do, too.

When we were little we knew that nothing *very* bad could happen with Mom or Dad there.

You know, we kind of still believe that.

LaDell

We went to the ocean when I was seven.

It was the Pacific Ocean, and the waves were high and the shoreline was steep. Sharks came in close to land sometimes. All in all a scary kind of place for a little girl to be — who had never seen the ocean before.

So for the first couple of hours I just played around in the sand, far from the water. But there's something about the sea — it draws you in. The water would wash in with a roar, and then a rush of shallow water would tumble up the beach, fade into the sand, and wash back out as another swell of water pushed up toward me.

I stuck my toe in. It was cold. But within an hour of the first touch, I was out just beyond the reach of the high waves. And I wanted to go into them, too, because the fascination wasn't satisfied; but I was too afraid.

Dad hadn't pushed me to go into the water when I was still afraid of it, and the only hint I had that Mom noticed was that she commented on how dry I still was after my first few hours.

But as I stood there watching the waves, almost hypnotized — you know the feeling? — Dad and Mom came splashing out to me and picked me up, holding me high in the air over the waves. And they walked right out into the breakers.

Now I realize the breakers were really rather low — they broke at Dad's waist level. But to me they were very high. And as I hung in Mom's and Dad's arms over the rushing water, I had a terrible feeling of vertigo and I started to scream and cry and insisted that they take me back to the beach.

If they had, I probably would have been afraid of waves all my life. Instead, Daddy took me and held me tight, really tight, with my face at his shoulder. Now the waves were coming in hitting *me,* and in a way it was even scarier. But not with Dad holding me. Because he swayed with the waves but never lost balance.

Then Mom began ducking under the waves and coming up on the other side, laughing and making funny faces. I laughed.

It was fun. And even though I was too small for Dad to let me stand alone in the breakers, he and Mom tossed me around in the water, held me as if I were surfing. It was wonderful.

And always their hands held me and I knew I was safe.

Years later, when I gained my testimony of Jesus, I thought back and realized that the safe, good, secure feeling I have with the Lord in control of my life was the same kind of feeling I had as a little child, entrusting my life to my father's hands. To my mother's arms.

Dave

The day I got the divorce — well, no, it was the day Cherie left. I came home from work and the house was empty and all her clothes were gone, and all her knick-knacks. The only things left were the gifts I had given her. And her diamond ring and the wedding band.

It was obvious what had happened, but I just stood there looking around for about an hour and a half, just noticing everything that was missing. The separation really was a surprise. We'd been having problems, drifting apart, but I didn't really think she'd ever leave me. Nobody I knew had ever *left*.

And then when it sank in, I didn't know what to do. I thought of trying to find Cherie, but who could I call? "Hi, Jerry, I'm trying to find my wife. Happen to know where she is? Yes, she took all her clothes, I think she may be planning on a long stay." Ha. No way would I do that. All I could do was accept the fact she was gone. At least, that's the way my mind worked then.

So I went downstairs and got in my car and drove two hundred miles. I got to my parents' house at about eleven o'clock that night. I came in and told them.

Their reactions were absolutely predictable. Mom and Dad were very, very calm. They asked about details ("Are you sure?" "Yes, I'm sure") and said things like "I'm sure she'll come back" and "You just wait, she'll find out how much she needs you."

I knew perfectly well how much she needed me. I also knew that I had failed her completely and that she knew better than to come back to me to satisfy her "needs." I was a lousy husband. I didn't deserve for her to come back. So I told them that.

Then Mother started to cry. "Where did I fail you?" she asked. "We never set a very good example." That was true, but I told them it wasn't true. Dad was more stoic. He just told me, "Life will go on, son."

They sounded like they were reciting lines from a very bad play.

So I started yelling at them. "You didn't fail me," I said. "I failed myself. I didn't come here to listen to you tell me that life'll go on and that you should have been a better example. I came here because Cherie's left me and I don't have anyplace else to go. Do you think I can face going to that lousy empty apartment?" I went on and on, pouring out my emotions, but yelling the whole time. I think I even threw things. I think I knocked over a lamp. I was doing all the yelling that in all my patient discussions with Cherie I had never cared enough to do.

In fact, it may have been the first time anybody ever yelled at anybody in my parents' house.

When I was through, Mom and Dad just sat there looking shocked. Then Dad walked to the closet and put on his coat. He unhung Mom's coat and held it out for her.

"Where are we going?" Mom asked.

"Get your coat, Dave," Dad said.

"Where are we going?" I asked.

"Out to the car," Dad said.

So we went out to the car, and Dad just drove. At about 3:00 A.M., with both Mom and me asleep, he stopped at a motel. We got out and went in.

The next day we got up at noon and went to a restaurant. Apparently Mom and Dad had found some time to talk about what they were doing, and they began to talk about things, crazy things. Wonderful things. Just ordinary tourist-talk. And I was so wiped out by the scene the night before and my worries about Cherie that I sat there, numb, listening to them.

I caught on fast to what they were trying to do, and my first impulse was to reject it, was to cut out and go back and try to handle my problems alone. But then I thought, Don't be a jerk, Dave. They're trying to help you get your mind off your problems, and off your problems is a good place to keep your mind.

So I joined in. And for three days we played tourist. Dad would just drive. Mom and I followed along on the road map, trying to guess where Dad was taking us. I couldn't believe some of the places we went. Towns that tourists never go to. But we found beautiful old lonely-looking houses. Little hills covered with sheep or cattle. Patches of old snow that the springtime hadn't been able to melt yet. Towns with ridiculous names. Greasy spoon restaurants with hilarious signs like "Eat here and get gas" (they had gas pumps out in front) and "Food that slides down easy" (they cooked everything in eight inches of old crankcase oil).

And Dad took pictures of everything. Every time we passed a road sign like "Welcome to Lower Podunk," Dad would pull over and Mom and I had to pose while he took a picture of us by the sign. I climbed up onto some of the signs, or stood on my head. The pictures turned out great, by the way.

At the end of the three days we were dirty and tired and our clothes looked like they'd never recover. They dropped me off at my apartment and said they'd have my little brother Lane drive my car back up to me.

I went back into my apartment and went right to bed. When I woke up I noticed right away that Cherie wasn't there, and I missed her. But I didn't feel lost. I didn't feel alone. Somebody loved me. What they did was so *obvious* that the cynic inside me would usually reject it. But this time I needed it, and let it happen, and they helped me, and it worked.

I wasn't afraid to go on. You know? The folks were there when I needed them, even if I had to beat them over the head to get them to realize my need!

Arlene

When I was a child I had terrible nightmares. I dreamed that my closet was full of large, indescribable shadows that came out of the darkness and sat on me and pressed me until I couldn't breathe. They smelled terrible — I've never met anybody else who smells things in their dreams, but I did. I can still remember the smell — every now and then something reminds me of it.

I would wake up screaming, and sure enough my closet really *was* full of dark shapes. I knew they were about to come out and get me again. And so I screamed and cried.

I remember that no matter how late at night it was, Mother was never angry or even irritated, or at least she never showed me. She just came padding in wearing furry slippers and a faded bathrobe and sat beside me. I clung to her and told her about the terrible things that came out of the closet. She got up and turned on the light, and went through the clothing hanging there, checking between every single piece of clothing to make sure there wasn't anything hiding there. I can't believe her patience. She did this every time. She'd reach up and touch the farthest corners of the closet to show there was nothing there. And then she'd shut the closet door and turn the light off and come back to me.

By then I'd be calmed down by her soft, rhythmic, repetitious actions and words, and I'd already be drifting off to sleep. She sat beside me then and stroked my head. Just lightly rubbed my forehead, until I fell asleep.

When I think of comfort, I think of a soft hand stroking my brow. I think of the padding of furry bedroom slippers on a linoleum floor. I think of Mother not just turning on the light and saying, "See, there's nothing to be afraid of," but rather reaching into all the dark corners beyond my sight, proving that there was nothing there, nothing to fear. And cool hands stroking my head, wiping away fear, bringing sleep.

I wrote a poem about that. Do you want me to read it to you? Too bad, I'm going to read it whether you want me to or not. That's one of the prices you have to pay for talking to a lonely person — they start reading to you out of their diary!

Here's the poem.

Mother, you deceive. You deceive:
You touch my eyes

And heal them so I do not see;
You make me wise
And help me sleep
As if the darkness weren't shadowy,
As if the night
Did not on claws and talons creep
Around me when you leave,
Taking with you all the softness, all the light.
But under all the blankets, I believe, I believe.

Todd

I always planned on a mission. I worked to get ready. I earned money. I was active in church. I served as a leader in every priesthood quorum I was in. I made my Eagle when I was fourteen. I prayed twice a day and got answers. I loved the Lord and I knew that the mission was his will for me.

But it's one thing to plan on a mission. It's another thing when the family drives you to Salt Lake City and takes you to that dismal building and says good-bye.

I went to South America, but in those days you didn't go straight to the LTM — that was before the big building was ready at BYU. So my parents drove me to that made-over school they use for a mission home. You want to know a coincidence? I went to that school for first grade. But it didn't feel like coming home at all!

I went in and reported that I was there. My hair passed inspection, and then there were two hours to kill before I had to go there to stay. We went to a candy store and had a treat. And then we just kind of walked around on Temple Square. I was being really giddy, really hyped-up and ready to go, the way most green missionaries are. Nothing was going to discourage *me*. Ever.

But then it was time, and we walked back over to the mission home. Mom cried and said good-bye to me at the car and then sat there because she always thinks she looks hideous when she cries and won't let anybody see her. So it was Dad who walked through the parking lot behind the building with me. There were some trees, and there weren't many people around.

For the first time it really hit me. Or rather, for the first time I *let* it hit me that I was saying good-bye to my parents for the last time in *two years*. I know, *after* your mission, it seems that the time flew by. But at the age of nineteen, I looked back and realized that two years before that I had just been beginning my senior year in high school. Two years was a long time. Two years was forever!

And I started to cry. I was full of the feeling of love for my parents, for my family, and full of emptiness — can you be full of emptiness? — at the thought of being gone so long. I missed them already. Actually, more at that moment than at any time on my mission.

So there I was in the parking lot with tears running down my cheeks and all the giddiness and braggadocio of a new missionary completely gone. Instead I was just a scared little boy.

Some guys have dads who would have gotten embarrassed and patted them on the back and said, "Buck up, kiddo, you've got to act like a man."

Instead my father reached down and took my hand. I was afraid to look at him because I was ashamed of the tears running down my cheeks. But I could feel his strong, dry, large hand holding mine, and I felt better. It made me cry a little harder for a minute. But that was all right.

And then, off in a corner of the parking lot, he stopped and turned to face me. I faced him, too, and was all ready to wipe my tears away until I realized that he was crying too, just as hard as I was. But he smiled at me, and hugged me, and kissed me on the cheek.

"I love you, Dad," I said.

"I love you, Todd," he said.

No big speech of good-bye. Just that. It was perfect. I wiped away the tears and went inside feeling full. Feeling strong.

I'm glad I had a father who knew when to hold my hand.

Listen, Mom and Dad:

When there's nothing else to hold to in this world, we hold on to you.

Listen, Mom and Dad . . .

Afterword: you've done a pretty good job

In this book I've painted the parents pretty clearly: Cathy's parents are repressive and punishing; Dave's parents are overly permissive; Todd's and LaDell's parents have done a pretty good job of raising their kids; Reuben's parents really didn't have a program at all — just let the family raise itself; and Arlene's parents had so many problems themselves that in spite of good intentions they really messed up her life.

Well, in real life people aren't all that clear-cut. Parents do some things wrong and some things right. They make mistakes, but they overcome them.

Remember, that in these examples all of the children are now active members of the Church, good people. Some of them had more help from their parents than others in getting to be that way. But all of the kids "turned out" all right.

That's an important thing to remember. Don't look at a rebellious teenager or an adult who has drifted away from the gospel and say, "See! We've failed! Our child has turned out wrong." Your kids haven't "turned out" anything at the age of seventeen or twenty-two or forty. Just because they've rejected some things that are important to you doesn't mean they'll always reject those things. Your teachings are still there inside them, waiting to come out.

Besides, the way your kids "turn out" is really up to them. They make choices, too — they aren't machines automatically responding to what you do.

But you *do* make a difference. The biggest single difference in your children's lives. And I hope that the stories in this book will help you to make that difference be a positive one.